Adorable
Desserts
to Crochet

Marie Clesse

Photography by Fabrice Besse

DOVER PUBLICATIONS
Garden City, New York

Acknowledgments

Thank you to Estelle Hamm, my editor, and Mélanie Jean, my agent. Estelle, Mélanie, it was once again a great joy to work with you, from our gourmet meetings to select the designs to the final stages of the book.

Thank you to all those who have labored at the birth of this book, notably Fabrice Besse, Sonia Roy, and Lucile Jouret.

Thank you to Mathilde Manceau and Clara Bourget for supporting me regularly regarding communication about my books.

Thanks again and always to DMC for our numerous partnerships, your quality yarns, and thank you to Charline Binckly for your superfast shipments!

Thank you to my friends and family who, along with me, have become enthused about the birth of these little cakes.

And a special thanks to my friend, Anne-Lise, stamp engraver, artisan of art, and creator of Rose de Biboun, for her advice and encouragement.

And a thousand thanks to you, who are passionate about crochet. I hope that this book will live up to your expectations.

THE YARNS

The publisher and the author thank DMC for the magnificent yarns that were used for the creation of the designs.

This Dover edition, first published in 2024, is a new English translation of *Adorables pâtisseries* by Marie Clesse, with photography by Fabrice Besse, published by Mango, Paris, France, in 2022. The original French work has been translated into English by Janet Ross Snyder.

ISBN-13: 978-0-486-85343-7
ISBN-10: 0-486-85343-8

Printed in China by Chang Jiang Printing Media Co., Ltd.
85343801   2024
www.doverpublications.com

Introduction

Welcome to my workshop! You won't find any whisks or rolling pins here, just crochet hooks and yarn!

In early 2021, I participated in a festive event on Instagram that brought together crochet designers from different nationalities around the theme of pastry. Even though I am not a very regular client of this type of shop, and I am not particularly fond of cooking, there I was, on the internet, looking for a pastry that would be sufficiently well-known and graphic enough to be reproduced in crochet. I come across a photo of raspberry cream puffs, and I was off and running. When the pattern was published, it was downloaded from my site more than 2,000 times in one week, from all over the world. And I received several messages asking me if I was planning to publish a book on that subject.

I adored working on the theme of fruits and vegetables for the book *Adorable Fruits and Vegetables to Crochet*, and, since its publication, I had wanted to complement it with another volume, and so the idea germinated. One year later, the result of my work is in your hands.

In this book you will find 16 designs and numerous variants. You will create these pastries in sewn versions, ideal for a toy tea set or as gourmet decorations. You can even crochet them in a "some assembly required" version, to provide hours of engaging play for your children.

On your mark, get set, let's make pastries!

Marie

Contents

P. 36

Macarons

P. 38

P. 40

Napoleons

P. 42

Cookies

P. 43

P. 44

Pancakes

P. 45

Rainbow Layer Cake

P. 46

Blueberry and Strawberry Tarts

P. 52

Raspberry and Blackberry Tarts

P. 51

Fruit Tarts

P. 58

Materials

YARNS

The designs in this book have been crocheted with DMC Happy Cotton yarn, which I find perfect for *amigurumi*. You can easily find this yarn in stores or online shops.

For each design, you will find the yarn and thread colors used and the necessary quantities of each. However, feel free to use the yarn of your choice. If you choose another yarn, you must make sure to use a smaller crochet hook than the one recommended on the yarn ball. That way you can avoid having holes between the stitches and won't see the stuffing through the holes.

If you are a beginner, make sure to choose a yarn that is tightly spun. A yarn that splits can be very frustrating for a beginner (or even for a seasoned crocheter). In general, you are better off working with good quality yarns. They make the work much more pleasant.

If you want to make the designs a little smaller, you can use DMC Natura Just Cotton and crochet it with a 2.25mm or even a 2mm crochet hook, according to the suppleness desired.

CROCHET HOOKS

This table shows the correspondence between metric crochet hook sizes, US sizes, and UK sizes.

Metric	US	US Steel	UK	UK Steel
2mm	0	4	14	2½
2.25mm	B-1	2	13	1½
2.5mm	B-1 or C-2	2 or 1	13 or 12	1½ or 1
4mm	G-6		8	

To crochet the designs in this book, I have mainly used a 2.25mm crochet hook. I tend to crochet tightly, with small crochet hooks. If you are not comfortable with the size recommended, you can absolutely use a 2.5mm crochet hook. Your creations will thus be a little bigger and the stitches will be a little more spaced out. However, I don't recommend using a larger crochet hook with this weight of cotton, because the stitches will then be much more spaced out, and that would be more noticeable on designs of this size.

For certain designs, I have found it useful to have a slightly larger crochet hook (2.5mm). You can, however, absolutely do without one, as explained in the corresponding designs. A variant of the chocolate éclair also needs a 4mm crochet hook.

I cannot stress enough how important it is to invest in a good quality crochet hook. I prefer ergonomic crochet hooks, even though I hold my crochet hook in a nonstandard way, like a knife. But others may prefer a simple steel or aluminum hook. Do not hesitate to test a crochet hook design before launching into the purchase of a complete set. A good crochet hook should slide easily between the stitches, and its point must not get caught on the threads, to avoid splitting them.

STUFFING

I use polyester stuffing, treated for dust mites. It is easy to buy online, in 300g (10oz), 500g (1lb), or 1kg (2lb) bags. You can also find it in yarn shops, craft stores, or fabric stores, or in a pinch, you can reuse the stuffing from a pillow! It is difficult to indicate the quantity you will need for each design, because it all depends on whether you prefer to stuff lightly or firmly.

The stuffing must be dense enough to give a good shape to the project, but not so dense that it spreads out the stitches; if you stuff too densely, you will see the stuffing between each stitch, which is not pleasing and might even prove dangerous for young children.

• Embroidery thread. I use DMC Pearl Cotton, size 5.
• Wool effect plush yarn in polyester ($^{22}/_{25}$oz–93yd [25g–85m]). I use Baby Smiles Lenja Soft, from Schachenmayr.
• Yarn needle and a finer needle for the Pearl Cotton threads.
I also find it very useful to have a long needle (9cm–3½in) to pull the yarns through the stuffing for the largest pieces.
• Pins to hold the pieces together while assembling them.
• Stitch markers. If you don't have any, you can also use a small safety pin, a paper clip, or a small piece of thread passed through the stitch to mark it.
• Scissors.
• Flat pliers. They are very useful for stuffing the small crocheted parts, for adding a bit of stuffing to a precise location, or for pulling a needle through several thicknesses of wool and stuffing (and for saving your fingers).
• Textile glue or a glue gun. Hot glue works very well on textiles, but I prefer textile glue in a tube with a brush applicator. It is much easier to measure and distribute, there is no chance of getting burned, and the glue is much slower to set, which gives you time to adjust or correct the alignment of the pieces to be glued.

• Thin plastic or cardboard. To obtain a base or a top that is nicely flat for certain designs, we will use a disc cut from a piece of plastic. Personally, I use plastic of about $^1/_{25}$in (1mm) in thickness, sold by the length desired in hobby shops under the name "Multiglass Cristal." It is easy to cut with scissors and rigid enough to remain flat in spite of the stuffing. You can also use the covers of carry-out food packaging, which will be perfect for this use. If plastic is not available, you can use rigid cardboard. This would be perfectly adequate for designs "for display only." However, if your creations will be used by children, I advise you to use plastic, which will make your toys more durable and easier to wash!
• Optional: pipe cleaners (chenille stem).

The following explanations are given for those who hold the crochet hook in the right hand. If you are left-handed, you must follow the explanations using a mirror image.

THE BASIC STITCHES

Chain stitch (ch): stitches in the air

1. Make a slip knot: insert the crochet hook in the loop of the knot; then, using the point of the hook, catch the yarn coming from the ball or skein and bring it back through the loop. This slip knot is the starting point, but it never counts as a stitch.
2. To make a chain stitch (ch), yarn over (pass the yarn from back to front, over the crochet hook) and bring this yarn through the loop of the hook.
3. Repeat the second step until you obtain the desired number of stitches. The loop on the crochet hook must never be counted.

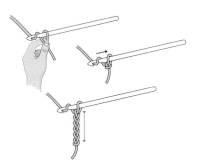

Slip stitch (sl st)

1. Insert the crochet hook in the stitch indicated.
2. Yarn over (yo) and bring the yarn through the stitch where the hook is and through the loop on the crochet hook. There should be one loop left on the crochet hook.

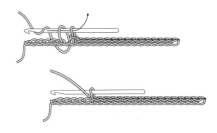

Single crochet (sc)

1. Insert the crochet hook into the stitch indicated.
2. Yarn over and bring the yarn through the stitch where your hook is. There should be two loops left on the hook.
3. Yarn over a second time and bring the yarn through the two loops. There should be one loop left on the crochet hook.

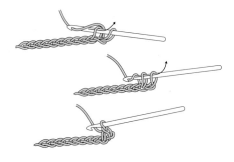

Half double crochet (hdc)

1. Yarn over, then insert the crochet hook into the stitch indicated.

2. Yarn over a second time and bring the yarn through the stitch where your hook is. There should be three loops on the crochet hook.

3. Yarn over one last time and bring the yarn through the three loops. There should be one loop left on the crochet hook.

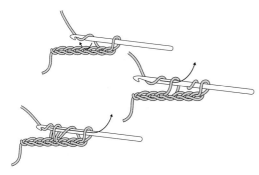

Double crochet (dc)

1. Yarn over, then insert the crochet hook into the stitch indicated.

2. Yarn over a second time and bring the yarn back through one loop. There should be three loops left on the crochet hook.

3. Yarn over a third time and bring the yarn back through two loops. There should be two loops on the crochet hook.

4. Yarn over one last time and bring the yarn back through the two loops. There should be one loop left on the crochet hook.

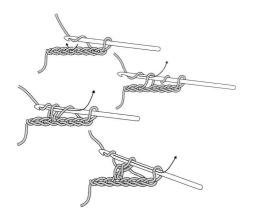

Treble crochet (tr)

1. Yarn over twice, then insert the crochet hook into the stitch indicated.

2. Yarn over a third time and bring the yarn back through the stitch where the crochet hook is. There should be four loops on the crochet hook.

3. Yarn over a fourth time and bring the yarn back through two loops. There should be three loops on the crochet hook.

4. Yarn over a fifth time and bring the yarn back through two loops. There should be two loops left on the crochet hook.

5. Yarn over one last time and bring the yarn back through the two loops. There should be one loop on the crochet hook.

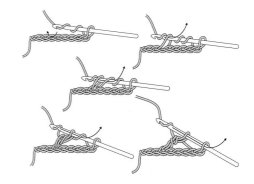

WHERE DO I INSERT THE CROCHET HOOK?

Unless otherwise indicated, always insert the hook from the front to the back.

In a chain

Insert the crochet hook into the upper loops of the chain. At the end of the chain, turn the work to the other side if you are crocheting in rows, or continue crocheting around the end of the chain to form an oval. In this case, continue crocheting on the chain, but this time in the lower loops.

In the stitches of a preceding row

The top of a crocheted stitch always has two small loops forming a horizontal V, no matter what type of stitch you are making. Unless you are instructed otherwise, always insert the crochet hook under both of these loops.

In the front loop only (FLO)

When this instruction is given, insert the crochet hook only in the front loop; that is, the loop of the V that is closest to you, on the front side of the work.

In the back loop only (BLO)

When this instruction is given, insert the crochet hook only in the back loop, that is, the loop of the V that is farthest away from you, on the back side of the work.

Around a stitch (relief stitch in front or in back)

To make a relief stitch in front or in back, we don't insert the crochet hook under the upper loops of a stitch, but slightly below, in the space between two stitches.

Relief stitch in front

Yarn over. Insert the crochet hook from the front to the back, in the space to the right of the stitch, then bring it out to the left of this stitch, from the back to the front. Continue the stitch in the usual way: yarn over, bring the yarn around the stitch; yarn over and bring the yarn under the first two loops on the crochet hook; yarn over again and bring the yarn through the two loops remaining on the crochet hook.

Relief stitch in back

Yarn over. Insert the crochet hook from the back to the front, in the space to the right of the stitch, then bring it out to the left of this stitch, from the front to the back. Continue the stitch in the usual way.

CROCHETING IN ROWS

Working in rows always starts with a chain that serves as a base. Crochet from right to left, turning the work (clockwise) at the end of each row. The last stitch crocheted thus becomes the first stitch of the next row. Working in rows makes it necessary to start with one or more chain stitches at the start of each row, depending on the height of the stitches that make up the row (which will be indicated in the instructions for the designs concerned).

CROCHETING IN THE ROUND

Working in the round (rnd) is the technique that is most often used to make *amigurumi*. It makes it possible to work continuously, without turning the work.

Working in the round starts by making a magic circle (or a chain if you want to make an oval piece), and then you can work in a spiral, or you can close each round with a slip stitch.

Simple magic circle

This technique makes it possible to tighten the first round so that there is no hole at the center of the work. Hold the end of the yarn between the thumb and index finger of your left hand. Wrap it around your index finger making one turn. Hold the part of the yarn connected to the ball with the middle finger and the ring finger. Insert the crochet hook under the loop formed on the index finger (between the yarn and the underside of your finger) and bring back the yarn attached to the ball. Make a chain stitch. The center ring is ready. Starting from there, crochet the number of stitches indicated in the loop thus formed. All that is left to do is to pull the end of the yarn to tighten the circle. Secure this yarn, if necessary, by crocheting it into the stitches of the second round.

Crocheting in a spiral

This technique consists of crocheting continuously, without closing the rounds.

At the end of a round, simply continue crocheting in the next stitch, which is the first stitch of the round that you just finished.

It is important to use a stitch marker to keep your place in your work. Place this marker on the first stitch of each round. On the last stitch of the round, remove the marker, make the first stitch of the following round, and place the marker over it.

Crocheting in closed rounds

This technique consists of closing each round before moving on to the following one.

After making the last stitch of the round, make a slip stitch in the first stitch that you made at the start of the round. This stitch closes the round, and it is never counted in the stitch count of the round.

To start a new round, first make the number of chain stitches corresponding to the type of stitch that you are going to crochet on this round, to reach the correct height: one chain for single crochet, two for half double crochet, three for double crochet, etc. When you work in closed rounds, this chain is not counted in the stitch count for the round. Next, make the first stitch of the new round in the first stitch of the preceding round (the same one as the one in which you just made a slip stitch).

Even though it is easier to keep your place in the work by crocheting in this manner, I advise you to mark the first stitch of each round all the same.

I am often asked why I crochet certain parts in closed rounds in the designs. It is, in fact, more common to crochet *amigurumi* in a spiral. Crocheting in closed rounds has its advantages. First of all, it makes color changes clearer for a striped design. For certain pieces, it also makes it possible to have a result that is straighter or more level. However, if you are having difficulty with this technique, it is quite possible to crochet in a spiral instead.

Trick: It is easy to make the demarcation that is formed with the slip stitch to close each round almost invisible. All you have to do is tighten this stitch to the maximum, while crocheting the rest normally!

INCREASES

An increase consists of simply making two stitches in the same stitch of the preceding round or row. The *amigurumi* or other crocheted objects are made essentially with single crochet. Also, when you see the abbreviation "inc," it means that you must make two single crochets in the same stitch.

It sometimes happens that you must increase another type of stitch. In this case, the instruction will be "two half double crochets in the same stitch." You may also be instructed to make "three single crochets in the same stitch." Follow the instructions exactly to obtain the expected results.

DECREASES

A decrease consists of crocheting two stitches together to obtain only one stitch in that place. I mainly use the technique of invisible decreases. When you find the abbreviation "dec," it means that you must crochet two single crochets together. To do that, instead of inserting the crochet hook under both loops of the stitch, insert it in the front loop of the stitch, then immediately insert it in the front loop of the following stitch. Next make a single crochet. If you must make a decrease in a half double, follow the same method: yarn over as you would do for a normal half double, then insert the crochet hook in the front loop of the first stitch and immediately afterward in the front loop of the following stitch. Yarn over again, bring the yarn back through these two front loops. Then yarn over again and bring the yarn back through the three loops on the crochet hook.

To decrease the number of stitches of a round, it is sometimes necessary to flow the stitches together. This consists of making incomplete stitches (you do not make the last yarn over of these stitches), in order to flow them together when you make the final, common yarn over. For example, to flow two single stitches together, you must follow these steps:

• Insert the crochet hook as indicated in the following stitch, yarn over, and bring back the yarn. At this point, there are two loops on the crochet hook.

• Instead of finishing this single stitch, insert the crochet hook in the following stitch, yarn over, and bring back the yarn. There are now three loops on the crochet hook.

• Do a last yarn over and bring back the yarn through the three loops on the crochet hook. Now there is only one loop on the hook. To flow together another type of stitch, always proceed in the same manner by following all the steps of the stitch in question, except for the last yarn over. After having made the number of incomplete
stitches to flow together (there can be more than two of them), do a last yarn over and bring back the yarn through all the loops on the crochet hook.

It is important to do a color change at the moment indicated in order to obtain the desired result. But, to obtain a neat result, you must start at the previous stitch!

To do this, when you crochet the last stitch before the color change, follow these steps:

• Start the single crochet normally. Insert the crochet hook, yarn over, and pull the yarn toward the stitch. You now have two loops on the crochet hook.

• Change the color at that moment by doing a yarn over with the new color, and bring this yarn through the two loops on the hook. There is now one loop of the new color on the crochet hook.

Next, continue to crochet with this new color. Make a knot on the back of the work with the ending yarn of the old color and the starting yarn of the new color. Sometimes you have to make repeated color changes. In this case, it is preferable not to cut the old color yarn, but to keep it attached so that you can start to crochet with it again a few stitches later or in the next round.

RIGHT SIDE OR WRONG SIDE OF THE STITCHES?

It is sometimes difficult for beginners to figure out which is the right side or the wrong side of their work. If you are right-handed, when you insert the crochet hook from the front to the back (that is, from the outside to the inside as the piece begins to take its rounded shape), the right side of the work is toward you (that is, the outside as the piece begins to take shape).

For pieces crocheted in the round, it is easier to crochet if you keep the right side of the work to the outside. You can choose to keep the back side visible for aesthetic reasons, but that presents two difficulties. First, the back side of the work is more disorganized. The back side of single stitches presents a succession of little horizontal features that form lines, and the stitches are more difficult to see and to count. The right side of single stitches forms little Vs that are much easier to count. The major issue with the back side of the work is that it is more difficult

to make invisible decreases there. Depending on the project the decreases will be much more visible, and the finished product will be less attractive.

Train yourself to tell the front from the back with a few rounds of single crochet, and then observe the difference by testing other types of stitches!

FINISHING TECHNIQUES

Clean finishes are very important for an attractive result. Here is how to stop and close the various crocheted pieces.

Stopping the yarn invisibly

When you work in a spiral, without closing the rounds, you obtain a sort of stairstep—the edge is not clean. To improve the uneven edge, the instructions will ask you to finish with a slip stitch.

Cut the yarn to about 6in (15cm) and thread a needle with it. Skip over the following stitch and pass the needle under the next two back loops, going from the inside to the outside of the piece. Then pass the needle under the back loop of the slip stitch, by inserting it toward the inside of the piece.

Make a knot on the back side of the work, or keep the length of the yarn for sewing, according to the instructions given. This technique reproduces the two loops of a stitch above the stitch that you skipped. That makes it possible to obtain a clean result without having to change the number of stitches.

Closing a piece

After making the last stitch, cut the yarn off at about 8in (20cm). With a needle, pass the yarn under the front loop of the following stitch, from the inside toward the outside. Do the same with all the stitches of the last crocheted round (generally 5 or 6 stitches). Then pull the yarn to close the opening.

Pass this yarn through the central hole and bring it out the other side of the crocheted piece. Adjust the tension so that it is well closed, but not enough to crush the piece. Pass the yarn through the piece once or twice more to secure the closure. Cut the yarn off flush with the surface of the piece.

ASSEMBLY

Sewing two open pieces together, edge to edge

When the last rounds of the two pieces have the same number of stitches, simply pass the thread alternatively through one stitch of the first piece (from the inside toward the outside) and then through a stitch of the second piece (from the outside to the inside). After making the last stitch, make several more stitches to secure the closure and then cut the thread off flush with the surface of the piece.

Sewing an open piece to a closed piece

Position the piece to be sewn at the desired place and pin it there so it does not move. You must sew all the stitches of the last round to obtain a good-looking finish. Insert the needle under a thread of the closed piece, and then over the two loops of the stitch of the last round, from the inside toward the outside. Repeat this operation to sew all the stitches. Before doing the last stitches, add a little stuffing, if necessary. Bring the yarn to the inside several times and cut it off flush with the surface.

EMBROIDERY

Several designs indicate to embroider elements. If you know exactly where to place them, you can embroider before stuffing the piece and simply make a knot on the back side of the work. However, it is often difficult to evaluate the correct placement before stuffing. To embroider the elements after stuffing, take a long, fine needle and insert it between two stitches at the back of the piece, or in the stuffing through the opening of the piece, and bring it back out at the place where the embroidery should go. Embroider the elements, then bring the thread back out exactly where it went in at the back of the piece, or through the stuffing again. Make a knot with the two threads, then push the knot inside the piece to make it invisible. With a needle, if necessary, push the two ends inside and cut off any part that is still sticking out.

SOME ADVICE BEFORE STARTING

To produce smooth work, do not tighten the stitches too much. The crochet hook should be able to pass easily through the stitches, and you should always keep the same tension on your yarn. If you are a beginner, practice making the basic stitches before starting the first design. That will help you feel at ease with the various basic stitches and their abbreviations, and you will not be obliged to constantly refer to the *Techniques* chapter of the book.

Feel free to vary the size of the crochet hook depending on the way you crochet: If you crochet more loosely, you may benefit from using a smaller crochet hook. On the other hand, if you tend to crochet more tightly, you may want to choose a larger crochet hook.

Read the instructions for a design completely before beginning to make sure that you understand everything and that you have not overlooked important information. The estimated time it takes to make each design has been provided as a rough guide, but may vary according to your crocheting experience. The duration indicated includes the time I spend reading the instructions as I go and crocheting at a relaxed speed.

Attention! Certain small designs are not appropriate for children younger than three years old and present choking hazards. If you make the designs with the yarns indicated in this book, do not leave them within reach of young children.

ABBREVIATIONS

BL = back loop
BLO = in the back loop only
bo = bobble stitch
ch = chain stitch(es)
dc = double crochet(s)
dec = invisible decrease
hdc = half double crochet(s)
inc = increase
rnd(s) = round(s)
row(s) = row(s)
sc = single crochet(s)
st = stitch(es)
sl st = slip stitch(es)
tr = treble crochet
( ) x 6 = crochet items in the parentheses six times
(6 st) = number of stitches for each round

Charlotte Russe

Dimensions
Approximate size:
2¾in x 2½in (7cm x 6cm)

Materials
› One 2.25mm crochet hook
› DMC Happy Cotton (¾oz–47 yd [20g–43m]), shade 787, vanilla, 1oz (28g); shade 764, pale pink, ²/₅oz (12g); **Raspberry:** shade 755, raspberry, ¹/₂₅oz (1g); **Blackberry + blueberry:** shade 758 navy blue, ⁷/₁₀₀oz (2g); **Strawberries:** shade 789, red, ³/₂₀oz (4g); shade 781, malachite green, 2¼yd (2m)
› DMC Pearl Cotton, size 5, white, 1⅛yd (1m) (for the strawberries)
› Small sheet of plastic or cardboard: about 4in x 2in (10cm x 5cm).
See the *Materials* chapter, p. 23, for more information.

CENTRAL PIECE

1st part
In pale pink. Crochet in the round, in closed rounds.
The sl st that closes each rnd and the ch that starts each rnd are not indicated in the instructions, for easier readability, but you must do them for each rnd. For more instructions, see the *Techniques* chapter, p. 24.
Rnd 1: 6 sc in a magic circle (6 st).
Rnd 2: 6 inc (12 st).
Rnd 3: (1 sc, 1 inc) x 6 (18 st).
Rnd 4: (1 sc, 1 inc, 1 sc) x 6 (24 st).
Rnd 5: (3 sc, 1 inc) x 6 (30 st).
Rnd 6: (2 sc, 1 inc, 2 sc) x 6 (36 st).
Rnd 7: (5 sc, 1 inc) x 6 (42 st).
Mark the back loop of the 1st st of the rnd and close rnd 7 with 1 sl st. Cut the yarn to a length of 16in (40cm).

2nd part
In pale pink. Crochet in the round, in closed rounds. The sl st that closes each rnd and the ch that starts each rnd are not indicated in the explanations, for easier readability, but you must make them for each rnd. For more instructions, see the *Techniques* chapter, p. 24.
Rnds 1 to 7: Repeat the instructions for the 1st part.

Do not cut the yarn and continue to crochet.
Rnd 8: In the back loop only (BLO): 42 sc (42 st).
Rnds 9 to 18: 42 sc (42 st).
Mark the last st of the rnd. Cut the yarn to a length of 4in (10cm), stop it invisibly, and tie a knot on the back side.

LADYFINGER X 10

In vanilla. Crochet in a spiral.
Rnd 1: 6 sc in a magic circle (6 st).
Rnd 2: (1 sc, 2 inc) x 2 (10 st).
Rnd 3: (1 sc, 1 inc, 3 sc) x 2 (12 st).
Stuff very lightly as you go along.
Rnds 4 to 14: 12 sc (12 st).
Rnd 15: 9 sc, 1 sl st, do not crochet the last 2 st (12 st).
Cut the yarn to a length of 6in (15cm). Flatten the piece so as to have the yarn at one end, and sew the two thicknesses edge to edge. To do that, insert the needle under the back loop of the last sc crocheted, from the outside of the ladyfinger toward the inside, then under the back loop of the st in which you made the last sl st, from the inside of the ladyfinger to the outside. Make 5 similar sewing st and then bring the yarn to the inside and cut it off flush with the surface.

Classics

BERRIES

Crochet 2 strawberries, 1 raspberry, 1 blackberry, and 1 blueberry, following the instructions given in the *Toppings* chapter, p. 59.

ASSEMBLY

With the yarns kept at the end of each berry, sew them to the 1st part of the central piece, in a pretty arrangement. Just make a few st to attach the strawberries, the raspberry, and the blueberry. Stuff the blackberry lightly and make a sewing st in each st of the last rnd. Tie the yarns in a knot on the back side of the 1st part of the central piece, and cut the yarns.

From the sheet of cardboard or plastic, cut two circles of the same diameter as the bottom of the central piece. Personally, I cut circles with a diameter of $1^4/_5$in (4.6cm), but this measurement will vary according to the size of the yarn and crochet hook, and according to how tightly or loosely you crochet.

Position one circle in the bottom of the central piece and keep the other one for the top.

Sew the 1st crocheted part to the 2nd part this way: with the yarn kept at the end of the 1st part, insert the needle under the 2 loops of the previously marked st on the 2nd part, from the outside to the inside; then insert the needle under the back loop marked on the 1st part, from the back side to the right side.

Sew like that for half the circumference.

Stuff the piece, and place the second circle under the 1st crocheted part. Finish the sewing, adding a little stuffing if necessary. Secure the yarn by making a few more st in the central piece, and then cut it off flush with the surface.

Finally, sew the ladyfingers around the central piece, with the rounded side toward the top. To make sure that they are well distributed around the piece, start by attaching them to each other. To do that, take 2 lengths of vanilla/Sundae yarn of about a yard long. Run the 1st yarn through the base of all the ladyfingers, between rnds 13 and 14, traversing them from side to side. Pass the 2nd yarn through the top of each ladyfinger, between rnds 4 and 5. Install the circle of ladyfingers around the central part, adjusting the tightness of the yarns that hold them together. With the remaining lengths of yarn and a long needle, cross the piece from ladyfinger to ladyfinger so as to attach the top and bottom of each ladyfinger to the central part. Make a few more st to secure the yarn and cut it off flush with the surface.

An alternative way to assemble: If you wish, you may attach the ladyfingers to each other to form a circle, but not sew it to the central part and not sew on the berries. The charlotte russe is thus transformed into a kit to be assembled.

French Strawberry Cake

Dimensions
Approximate
diameter: 3¼in (8cm)

Materials
› One 2.25mm crochet hook
› DMC Happy Cotton (¾oz–47yd [20g–43m]), shade 789, red, ¼oz (6g); shade 793, coral, ¹/₁₀oz (3g); shade 761, ecru, ½oz (16g); shade 781, malachite green, 3¼yd (3m)
› DMC Pearl Cotton, size 5, white, ½yd (50cm) per strawberry
› Small sheet of plastic or cardboard: about 6in x 3in (15cm x 7.5cm). See the *Materials* chapter, p. 23, for more information.

Preliminary information
There are numerous color changes in rnds 11 to 16.
Personally, I do not cut the yarns; I just bring them along on the back side of the piece. Make sure to untangle the yarn balls occasionally so that they don't end up in an enormous knot.

CAKE

1st part
In ecru. Crochet in the round, in closed rnds. The sl st that closes each rnd and the ch that starts each rnd are not indicated in the instructions, to make them more readable, but you must do them for every rnd. For more instructions, see the *Techniques* chapter, p. 24.
Rnd 1: 7 sc in a magic circle (7 st).
Rnd 2: 7 inc (14 st).
Rnd 3: (1 sc, 1 inc) x 7 (21 st).
Rnd 4: (1 sc, 1 inc, 1 sc) x 7 (28 st).
Rnd 5: (3 sc, 1 inc) x 7 (35 st).
Rnd 6: (2 sc, 1 inc, 2 sc) x 7 (42 st).
Rnd 7: (5 sc, 1 inc) x 7 (49 st).
Rnd 8: (3 sc, 1 inc, 3 sc) x 7 (56 st).
Rnd 9: (7 sc, 1 inc) x 7 (63 st).
Rnd 10: (4 sc, 1 inc, 4 sc) x 7 (70 st).
Mark the back loop of the 1st st of the rnd and close Rnd 10 with 1 sl st. Cut the yarn to a length of 20in (50cm).

2nd part
In ecru. Crochet in the round, in closed rnds. The sl st that closes each rnd and the ch that starts each rnd are not indicated in the instructions, to make them more readable, but you must do them for every rnd. For more instructions, see the *Techniques* chapter, p. 24.
Rnds 1 to 10: Repeat the instructions from the 1st part.
Do not cut the yarn.
To have a crisp and clear result, change the color, going to red, while making the sl st that closes rnd 10. The ch that starts rnd 11 is thus done in red.
Rnd 11: Crochet this rnd in the back loop only: in red: 2 sc, (in coral: 1 sc, in red: 2 sc, in coral: 1 sc, in red: 3 sc) x 9; in coral: 1 sc, in red: 2 sc, in coral: 1 sc, in red: 1 sc (70 st).
Rnd 12: In red: 2 sc, (in coral: 1 sc, in red: 2 sc, in coral: 1 sc, in red: 3 sc) x 9, in coral: 1 sc, in red: 2 sc, in coral: 1 sc, in red: 1 sc (70 st).
For a crisp and clear result, the color changes at the ends of rnds 12 to 16 are to be done when making the last sc of the rnd, which means that the sl st that ends the rnd and the ch that starts the next rnd are to be done in ecru.
Rnd 13: (In ecru: 1 sc, in red: 1 sc, in coral: 1 sc, in red: 2 sc, in coral: 1 sc, in red: 1 sc) x 10 (70 st).
Rnd 14: (In ecru: 2 sc, in red: 1 sc, in coral: 1 sc, in red: 1 sc, in coral: 1 sc, in red: 1 sc) x 10 (70 st).

Classics

Rnd 15: (In ecru: 3 sc, in red: 1 sc, in coral: 2 sc, in red: 1 sc) x 10 (70 st).
Cut the coral yarn.
Rnd 16: (In ecru: 4 sc, in red: 3 sc) x 10 (70 st).
Cut the red yarn.
Rnd 17: In ecru: 70 sc (70 st).
Mark the last st of the rnd. Cut the ecru yarn to a length of 4in (10cm), stop it invisibly, and tie a knot on the back side. Tie knots in the starting and ending coral and red yarns and cut them off.

STRAWBERRIES

Crochet 3 strawberries by following the instructions given in the *Toppings* chapter, p. 59.

ASSEMBLY

With the lengths of yarn kept at the end of each strawberry, sew them to the 1st part of the central piece, arranged in a pleasing manner. Just make a few st to attach each strawberry. Tie the yarns on the back side of the 1st part of the cake and cut the yarns.

From the sheet of cardboard or plastic, cut two circles of the same diameter as the bottom of the cake. Personally, I cut circles 2¾in (7.2cm) in diameter, but this measurement should be adapted to the yarn and crochet hook chosen, and according to they way you crochet, whether more or less loose.
Position one circle at the bottom of the cake and set the other one aside for the top.
Sew the 1st crocheted part to the 2nd part like this: with the yarn kept at the end of the 1st part, insert the needle under the 2 loops of the previously marked st on the 2nd part, from the outside to the inside, then insert the needle under the back loop marked on the 1st part, from the back side to the front.
Sew like that for half the circumference.
Stuff the cake, and place the second circle under the 1st crocheted part. Finish the sewing, adding a little stuffing if necessary.
Bring the yarn to the inside by making several st in the cake and cutting it off flush with the surface.

Éclairs

 p. 8

1 hour 30 minutes to 2 hours 15 minutes

Dimensions
Approximate
length: 4in (10cm)

Materials
› One 2.25mm crochet hook and one 4mm crochet hook (for the variant in coconut)
› DMC Happy Cotton (¾oz–47yd [20g–43m]), **in common**: shade 776, camel, ²/₅oz (11g); **Chocolate**: shade 777, chocolate, ¹/₅oz (5g); **Raspberry**: shade 799, bubblegum pink, ¹/₅oz (5g); shade 755, raspberry, ¹/₁₀oz (2g); **Lemon**: shade 788, lemon, ¹/₅oz (5g); shade 762, white, ¹/₁₀oz (2g)
› Wool effect plush yarn in polyester (²²/₂₅oz–93yd [25g–85m]), shade white, ¹/₁₀oz (3g) (for the variant in coconut)
› Optional: pipe cleaner (chenille stem), 6in (15cm)

CHOCOLATE ÉCLAIR

Choux pastry
In camel. Crochet in a spiral around a starting chain.

Rnd 1: Ch 20; in the 2nd st away from the crochet hook: 1 inc; continuing along the ch: 17 sc; in the last st of the chain: 3 sc; coming back up the other side of the ch: 18 sc (40 st).
Rnd 2: 2 inc, 17 sc, 3 inc, 17 sc, 1 inc (46 st).
Rnd 3: (1 sc, 1 inc) x 2, 17 sc, (1 sc, 1 inc) x 3, 18 sc, 1 inc (52 st).
Rnd 4: (1 inc, 2 sc) x 2, 17 s c, (1 inc, 2 sc) x 3, 17 sc, 1 inc, 2 sc (58 st).
Rnd 5: (2 sc, 1 inc, 1 sc) x 2, 17 sc, (2 sc, 1 inc, 1 sc) x 3, 19 sc, 1 inc, 1 sc (64 st).
Rnds 6 and 7: 64 sc (64 st).
Rnd 8: (2 sc, 1 dec, 1 sc) x 2, 17 sc, (2 sc, 1 dec, 1 sc) x 3, 19 sc, 1 dec, 1 sc (58 st).
Rnd 9: (1 dec, 2 sc) x 2, 17 sc, (1 dec, 2 sc) x 3, 17 sc, 1 dec, 2 sc (52 st).
Rnd 10: (1 sc, 1 dec) x 2, 17 sc, (1 sc, 1 dec) x 3, 18 sc, 1 dec (46 st).
Rnd 11: 2 dec, 17 sc, 3 dec, 17 sc, 1 dec (40 st).
Rnd 12: 1 sl st, do not crochet the other st of the rnd (40 st).

Cut the yarn to a length of 12in (30cm) and start to stuff the two ends of the éclair.

Sew the two sides edge to edge to close the éclair. Start by inserting the needle under the front loop of the next st, from the inside to the outside. Next, sew the st face to face: insert the needle under the 2 loops of the next to last st of the rnd, from the outside to the inside, then under the 2 loops of the 2nd st of the rnd, from the inside to the outside. Sew like that for the entire length, stuffing as you go along.
Bring the yarn to the inside and cut it off flush with the surface.

Icing
In chocolate. Crochet in a spiral around a starting chain.
Rnds 1 to 5: Repeat the instructions for rnds 1 to 5 of the Choux pastry.
Cut the yarn to a length of 32in (80cm) and stop it invisibly.
Position the icing over the choux pastry and pin it in place, then sew each st of the last rnd of the icing to the pastry. Bring the yarn to the inside and cut it off flush with the surface.

VARIANTS

Strawberry éclair
Following the instructions above, crochet the choux pastry in camel and the icing in bubblegum pink, and sew on the icing.

Classics

Crochet 2 raspberries following the instructions given in the *Toppings* chapter, p. 59.
Sew the raspberries on the icing with a few st, then bring the thread to the inside and cut it off flush with the surface.

Lemon éclair
Following the instructions above, crochet the choux pastry in camel and the icing in lemon, and sew the icing onto the pastry.
Crochet 3 tubes of meringue following the instructions below.
In white. Crochet in a spiral.
Rnd 1: 5 sc in a magic circle (5 st).
Rnd 2: 5 sc in the back loop only (5 st).
Rnds 3 to 8: 5 sc (5 st).
Rnd 9: 4 sc, 1 sl st (5 st).
Optional: Use a pipe cleaner to stiffen the tube. Take a pipe cleaner and fold back one end using pliers. Measure the length necessary, fold back the 2nd end, and cut. Insert the pipe cleaner in the tube. Cut the white yarn to a length of 8in (20cm) and close the tube.

Position the meringue tubes on the éclair and overlap them. Make 1 sewing st on each end, and then pull the yarn to the inside and cut it off flush with the surface.

Coconut éclair
Following the instructions above, crochet the choux pastry in camel.
Use the wool effect plush yarn and a 4mm crochet hook to crochet the coconut icing, following the instructions below.
In white. Crochet in a spiral around a starting ch.
Rnd 1: Ch 13; starting in the 2nd st from the crochet hook: 1 inc; continuing along the ch: 10 sc; in the last st of the ch: 3 sc; coming back up the other side of the ch: 11 sc (26 st).
Rnd 2: 2 inc, 10 sc, 3 inc, 10 sc, 1 inc (32 st).
Rnd 3: (1 sc, 1 inc) x 2, 10 sc, (1 sc, 1 inc) x 3, 11 sc, 1 inc (38 st).
Rnd 4: (1 inc, 2 sc) x 2, 10 sc, (1 inc, 2 sc) x 3, 10 sc, 1 inc, 2 sl st (44 st).
Cut the yarn to a length of 32in (80cm), stop the yarn invisibly, and sew the icing onto the pastry.

Cream Puffs (Profiteroles)

Dimensions
Approximate
height: 3in (7.5cm)

Materials
› One 2.25mm crochet hook
› DMC Happy Cotton (¾oz–47yd [20g–43m]), **in common:** shade 776, camel, ½oz (16g); **Chocolate:** shade 777, chocolate, ⅓oz (8g); shade 761, ecru, 5½yd (5m); **Vanilla:** shade 761, ecru, ⅓oz (8g); shade 787, vanilla, 5½yd (5m)

UPPER PART

Choux pastry
In camel. Crochet in a spiral.
Rnd 1: 6 sc in a magic circle (6 st).
Rnd 2: 6 inc (12 st).
Rnd 3: (1 sc, 1 inc) x 6 (18 st).
Rnd 4: (1 sc, 1 inc, 1 sc) x 6 (24 st).
Rnd 5: (3 sc, 1 inc, 4 sc) x 3 (27 st).
Rnd 6: (8 sc, 1 inc) x 3 (30 st).
Rnds 7 and 8: 30 sc (30 st).
Rnd 9: (3 sc, 1 dec) x 6 (24 st).
Rnd 10: (1 sc, 1 dec, 1 sc) x 6 (18 st).
Start stuffing.
Rnd 11: (1 sc, 1 dec) x 6 (12 st).
Rnd 12: 6 dec (6 st).
Cut the yarn to a length of 12in (30cm) and finish stuffing.

Icing
In chocolate or ecru. Crochet in spiral.
Rnd 1: 6 sc in a magic circle (6 st).
Rnd 2: 6 inc. (12 st).
Rnd 3: (1 sc, 1 inc) x 6 (18 st).
Rnd 4: (1 sc, 1 inc, 1 sc) x 6 (24 st).
Rnd 5: (3 sc, 1 inc) x 6 (30 st).
Rnd 6: (1 sc, 1 hdc, 2 hdc in 1 st, 1 hdc, 2 sl st, 3 sc, 1 sl st) x 3 (33 st).
Cut the yarn to a length of 16in (40cm) and stop it invisibly.
Using pins, position the icing on the choux pastry, on the magic circle side. Sew each st of the last row of icing to the choux pastry. Bring the yarn to the inside and cut off even with the surface.

LOWER PART

Icing
In chocolate or ecru. Crochet in a spiral.
Rnd 1: 6 sc in a magic circle (6 st).
Rnd 2: 6 inc (12 st).
Rnd 3: (1 sc, 1 inc) x 6 (18 st).
Rnd 4: (1 sc, 1 inc, 1 sc) x 6 (24 st).
Rnd 5: (3 sc, 1 inc) x 6 (30 st).
Rnd 6: (2 sc, 1 inc, 2 sc) x 6 (36 st).
Rnd 7: (5 sc, 1 inc) x 6 (42 st).
Rnd 8: (3 sc, 1 inc, 3 sc) x 6 (48 st).
Rnd 9: (1 sc, 1 hdc, 4 dc, 1 hdc, 4 sl st, 1 hdc, 2 hdc in 1 st, 1 hdc, 2 sl st) x 3 (51 st).
Cut the yarn to a length of 32in (80cm) and stop it invisibly, keeping the length.
With the yarn kept at the end of the choux pastry of the upper part, sew the 6 st of the last rnd of the choux pastry on the 6 st of the 1st rnd of the icing of the lower part. Tie the yarn in a knot on the back side and cut it off.

Choux pastry
In camel. Crochet in a spiral.
Rnd 1: 8 sc in a magic circle (8 st).
Rnd 2: 8 inc (16 st).
Rnd 3: (1 sc, inc) x 8 (24 st).
Rnd 4: (1 sc, 1 inc, 1 sc) x 8 (32 st).
Rnd 5: (3 sc, 1 inc) x 8 (40 st).
Rnd 6: (2 sc, 1 inc, 2 sc) x 8 (48 st).
Rnd 7: (11 sc, 1 inc) x 4 (52 st).
Rnds 8 to 11: 52 sc (52 st).
Rnd 12: (11 sc, 1 dec) x 4 (48 st).
Rnd 13: (3 sc, 1 dec, 11 sc) x 3 (45 st).
Rnd 14: (10 sc, 1 dec, 3 sc) x 3 (42 st).

Classics

Rnd 15: (5 sc, 1 dec) x 6 (36 st).
Rnd 16: (2 sc, 1 dec, 2 sc) x 6 (30 st).
Rnd 17: (3 sc, 1 dec) x 6 (24 st).
Start stuffing.
Rnd 18: (1 sc, 1 dec, 1 sc) x 6 (18 st).
Rnd 19: (1 sc, 1 dec) x 6 (12 st).
Finish stuffing.
Rnd 20: 6 dec (6 st).
Close, pull the yarn to the inside and cut it off flush with the surface.

Using pins, position the icing on the side of the last rnds of the lower part of the choux pastry, aligning the magic circle of the icing with the closure of the choux pastry. Sew each st of the last rnd of the icing to the choux pastry. Bring the yarn to the inside and cut it off flush with the surface.

Cream

In ecru or vanilla. Crochet in rows.
Row 1: Make one chain of 71 ch, keeping 4in (10cm) of starting yarn; starting in the 2nd st away from the crochet hook: (2 sl st, 1 hdc, 2 dc, 1 hdc, 1 sl st) x 10; turn the work (70 st).

Between each sequence of dc and hdc, we thus have 3 sl st. In the 2nd row, we will make 1 st only in each sl st of the middle. That will make it possible to fold the sequences of dc like an accordion, so as to create a ruffle of cream. When working the 2nd row, make sure to fold the sequences of dc toward the back, so that the dc is on the outside.
Row 2: Ch 1, (1 sl st in the sl st in the middle, ch 1) x 9, 1 sl st in the last sl st, ch 1.
Cut the yarn to a length of 4in (10cm).
Straighten out the work so that all the standing st are on the same side, and encircle the cream puff with this cream between the 2 choux pastries. Tie the 2 ends of the yarn together, then bring the yarns inside the cream puff before cutting them off flush with the surface.

Macarons

Dimensions
Approximate size:
1¾in x 1in
(4.5cm x 2.5cm)

Combinations of colors used
The macarons in the photos were made with these shades (shell/filling):
Rose flavor: 764, pale pink and 761, ecru
Raspberry flavor: 799, bubblegum pink and 755, raspberry
Pistachio flavor: 779, apple green and 782, almond
Blackcurrant flavor: 795, lilac and 756, violet
Violet flavor: 756, violet and 761, ecru
Coffee flavor: 773, beige and 777, chocolate
Lemon flavor: 788, lemon and 770, lemonade yellow
Chocolate mint flavor: 785, turquoise and 770, lemonade yellow

Materials
› One 2.25mm crochet hook and one 2.5mm crochet hook (optional)
› DMC Happy Cotton (¾oz–47yd [20g–43m]), shell, ½oz (15g); filling, 5½yd (5m)

SHELL x 2
Crochet in a spiral with the 2.25mm crochet hook.
Rnd 1: 7 sc in a magic circle (7 st).
Rnd 2: 7 inc (14 st).
Rnd 3: (1 sc, 1 inc) x 7 (21 st).
Rnd 4: (1 inc, 2 sc) x 7 (28 st).
Rnd 5: (3 sc, 1 inc) x 7 (35 st).
Rnd 6: (1 inc, 4 sc) x 7 (42 st).
So as not to have the sl st too tight in rnd 7, I use a 2.5mm crochet hook. If you do not have a crochet hook that is bigger than the one you used to start the shell, you can simply make sure to crochet a little looser than usual.
Rnd 7: (1 dec in sl st, 4 sl st) x 7 (35 st).
Mark the back loop of the last st of rnd 7.
Cut the yarn to a length of 4in (10cm). Stop it invisibly and tie it in a knot on the back side.

FILLING
Crochet in a spiral with the 2.25mm crochet hook.
Rnd 1: 7 sc in a magic circle (7 st).
Rnd 2: 7 inc (14 st).
Rnd 3: (1 inc, 1 sc) x 7 (21 st).
Rnd 4: (2 sc, 1 inc) x 7 (28 st).
Rnd 5: (1 inc, 3 sc) x 7 (35 st).

Rnd 6: 1 sl st, do not crochet the other st of the rnd (35 st).
Cut the yarn to a length of 35in (90cm). Stop it invisibly and then pass it under the 2 loops of the false st thus created, from the back side to the front side.

ASSEMBLY
First sew the filling to one shell with the length of yarn kept at the end of the filling.
Place the interior of one shell against the filling and sew together the st of the last rnd of the filling with the back loops of the st of the last rnd of the shell.
Here's how to do it: insert the needle under the back loop of the previously marked st on the shell, from the back side to the front side. Then insert the needle in the filling, under the 2 loops of the st where the yarn is coming from, from the right side to the back side.
*Insert the needle under the 2 loops of the next st on the filling, but this time from the back side to the front side. Insert the needle under the back loop of the following st on the shell, from the back side to the front side. Finally, insert the needle

Classics

under the 2 loops of the same st of the filling, from the right side to the back side.* Continue the sewing by repeating the steps between * and *. By doing it this way, we keep the filling quite visible between the 2 shells.

Before making the last st, stuff the shell lightly, so that it is not too puffy.

Do not cut the yarn; use it to sew the 2nd shell to the filling, using the same technique. The fact that the filling is already sewn to the 1st shell does not get in the way of sewing the 2nd shell, because the 2 loops of the heads of the st of the last rnd of the filling remain easy to see.

Once the 2nd shell is stuffed and sewn, stop and cut the yarn.

Now crochet a ruffle on each shell of the macaron, by inserting the crochet hook in the loops before the st of rnd 7, which remained exposed when sewing the shells.

Insert the crochet hook in one of the front loops, aiming toward the top of the shell on which you are crocheting the ruffle.

Pull through a yarn of the same color as the shell, keeping 4in (10cm) of starting yarn. Starting in the next st, do as follows:

(1 sc, 1 sl st) x 17, 1 sc in the st in which you pulled the yarn through at the start of the rnd (35 st). Cut the yarn to a length of 4in (10cm) and stop it invisibly. Secure the 2 yarns and cut them off flush with the surface.

Raspberry and Cream Macaron

 4 hours

 p. 11

Dimensions
Approximate
diameter: 2¾in (7cm)

Materials
› One 2.25mm crochet hook and one 2.5mm crochet hook (optional)
› DMC Happy Cotton (¾oz–47yd [20g–43m]), shade 755, raspberry,
⅓oz (9g); shade 761, ecru, ¹⁄₁₀oz (2 g); shade 764, pale pink, ¾oz (22g);
shade 799, bubblegum pink, ¹⁄₁₀oz (2g)
› Small sheet of plastic or cardboard: about 5⅛in x 2⅝in (13cm x 6.5cm)
See the *Materials* chapter, p. 23, for more information.

CENTRAL PART

1st part

In pale pink. Crochet in a spiral with the 2.25mm crochet hook.
Rnd 1: 6 sc in a magic circle (6 st).
Rnd 2: 6 inc (12 st).
Rnd 3: (1 inc, 1 sc) x 6 (18 st).
Rnd 4: (1 sc, 1 inc, 1 sc) x 6 (24 st).
Mark the front loop of the last st of rnd 4.
Rnd 5: In the back loop only: (1 inc, 3 sc) x 6 (30 st).
Rnd 6: (2 sc, 1 inc, 2 sc) x 6 (36 st).
Rnd 7: (1 inc, 5 sc) x 6 (42 st).
Rnd 8: (3 sc, 1 inc, 3 sc) x 6 (48 st).
Rnd 9: (1 inc, 7 sc) x 6 (54 st).
Rnd 10: 1 sl st; do not crochet the other st of the rnd (54 st).
Cut the yarn to a length of 4in (10cm), stop it invisibly and tie it in a knot on the back side.

2nd part

In ecru. Crochet in a spiral with the 2.25mm crochet hook.
Pull a yarn through the front loop marked on the 1st part, inserting the crochet hook in the direction of the magic circle. Keep 4in (10cm) of starting yarn, and make ch 1. Crochet the 1st rnd in the front loops of rnd 4 of the 1st part, starting in the same st.
Rnds 1 to 4: 24 sc (24 st).
Rnd 5: 1 sl st, do not crochet the other st of the rnd (24 st).

Cut the yarn to a length of 16in (40cm). Tie a knot in the starting yarn on the back side of the 1st part and cut it off.

3rd part

In pale pink. Crochet in a spiral with the 2.25mm crochet hook.
Rnd 1: 6 sc in a magic circle (6 st).
Rnd 2: 6 inc (12 st).
Rnd 3: (1 inc, 1 sc) x 6 (18 st).
Rnd 4: (1 sc, 1 inc, 1 sc) x 6 (24 st).
Slide a small yarn of contrasting color under the 2 loops of the 1st st of rnd 4, as a point of reference.
Rnd 5: (1 inc, 3 sc) x 6 (30 st).
Rnd 6: (2 sc, 1 inc, 2 sc) x 6 (36 st).
Rnd 7: (1 inc, 5 sc) x 6 (42 st).
Rnd 8: (3 sc, 1 inc, 3 sc) x 6 (48 st).
Rnd 9: (1 inc, 7 sc) x 6 (54 st).
Rnd 10: 1 sl st; do not crochet the other st of the rnd (54 st).
Cut the yarn to a length of 4in (10cm), stop it invisibly and tie it in a knot on the back side.
Sew the 2nd part to the 3rd part using the ecru yarn that was set aside. Position the place of the 3rd part against the ecru tube, and sew the last ecru rnd around rnd 4 of the 3rd part, starting with the st previously marked with a contrasting yarn. Before doing the last sewing st, stuff the ecru tube. Tie the yarn in a knot on the back side of the 3rd part and cut it off.

SHELL x 2

In pale pink. Crochet in a spiral with the 2.25mm crochet hook.

Rnd 1: 6 sc in a magic circle (6 st).
Rnd 2: 6 inc (12 st).
Rnd 3: (1 inc, 1 sc) x 6 (18 st).
Rnd 4: (1 sc, 1 inc, 1 sc) x 6 (24 st).
Rnd 5: (1 inc, 3 sc) x 6 (30 st).
Rnd 6: (2 sc, 1 inc, 2 sc) x 6 (36 st).
Rnd 7: (1 inc, 5 sc) x 6 (36 st).
Rnd 8: (3 sc, 1 inc, 3 sc) x 6 (48 st).
Rnd 9: (1 inc, 7 sc) x 6 (54 st).
Rnd 10: (1 inc, 5 sc) x 9 (63 st).

To avoid sl st that are too tight in rnd 11, I use a 2.5mm crochet hook. If you don't have a crochet hook bigger than the one you used to start the shell, you can simply crochet a little looser than usual.

Rnd 11: (1 dec in sl st, 5 sl st) x 9 (54 st).

Cut the yarn to a length of 24in (60cm) and stop the yarn invisibly.

RASPBERRIES

Crochet 10 raspberries following the instructions given in the *Toppings* chapter, p. 59. For one of the raspberries, keep 10in (25cm) of yarn at the end for sewing.

ASSEMBLY

Sewing

From the sheet of cardboard or plastic, cut one circle of the same diameter as the pink pieces of the central part. Personally, I cut a circle 2⅓in (6cm) in diameter, but this measurement should be adjusted according to the yarn and crochet hook chosen, and according to the way you crochet, whether more or less loose.

Place the inside of one shell against one of the pink pieces of the central part so that you can sew them together. Insert the needle under the back loop of 1 st of the central part, from the right side to the wrong side, then under the 2 loops of the following sl st on rnd 11 of the shell, from the inside to the outside.

Continue sewing like that for half the circumference, then place the plastic or cardboard circle on the pink piece of the central part. Add a little stuffing between the circle and the shell. Finish sewing, adding a little stuffing at the end if necessary. Bring the yarn back to the inside by making a few st in the cake and cutting it off flush with the surface. Do the same thing to sew the 2nd shell on the 2nd pink piece of the central part.

RUFFLE x 2

With the 2.25mm crochet hook, crochet 1 ruffle on each shell of the macaron, inserting the hook in the front loops of the central part that remained visible while the shells were being sewn.

Insert the crochet hook in the front loops, pointing toward the center of the macaron.

Pull a pale pink yarn through, keeping 6in (15cm) of starting yarn. Starting in the next st, do the following:

(1 sc, 1 sl st) x 27 (54 st).

Cut the yarn to a length of 6in (15cm) and stop it invisibly. Pull the 2 yarns to the inside and cut them off flush with the surface.

FILLINGS

Set the raspberry with the trailing yarn aside, and pull a raspberry-colored yarn through the other 9 raspberries, at the level of rnd 5. Place these 9 raspberries around the central tube, positioning the open part against one of the shells. Tie a knot in the 2 ends of the yarn, making sure that all the berries are held close to each other without being crushed. Pull each end of the yarn into the closest raspberry and cut the yarn off flush with the surface.

To finish, place the raspberry on the top shell, with the open side visible, and make a few st. Pull the yarn to the inside and cut it off flush with the surface.

Napoleons

Dimensions
Approximate size:
1¾in x 3¼in (4.5cm x 8.5cm)

Preliminary information
This design uses the technique of surface crochet.

Materials
› One 2.25mm crochet hook
› DMC Happy Cotton (¾oz–47yd [20g–43m]), shade 761, ecru, ¹⁄₁₀oz (5g); shade 776, camel, ½oz (14g); shade 787, vanilla, ⅔oz (18g); shade 777, chocolate, 2¼yd (2m)
› Textile glue or hot glue

CAKE LAYER x 8

Crochet in rows. This piece is to be crocheted once in ecru, 3 times in camel, and 4 times in vanilla.
Row 1: Ch 12, keeping 4in (10cm) of starting yarn; 11 sc starting in the 2nd st away from the crochet hook; turn the work (11 st).
Rows 2 to 22: Ch 1; 11 sc; turn (11 st).
Row 23: Ch 1; 11 sc (11 st).
Make ch 1 to stop the piece and cut the yarn to a length of 4in (10cm). Work the starting and ending yarn in under a few st, and cut off flush with the surface.
Using chocolate yarn, make the designs on the ecru cake layer.
Insert the crochet hook between rows 1 and 2, in the 4th st of row 1. Pull the chocolate yarn through, keeping 4in (10cm) of starting yarn. Now insert the crochet hook one row higher (between rows 2 and 3), and make 1 sl st on the surface. Continue, making 20 more surface sl st until you have made a vertical line over the length of the ecru rectangle, which ends between rows 22 and 23.
Cut the yarn to a length of 20in (50cm).
Make another line in the same way, starting in st 8 of row 1.
Using the yarns kept at the end of each surface chain, embroider short diagonal lines on each side of each ch, following the design shown in the diagram.

Tie a knot in the yarns on the back side and cut them off.

ASSEMBLY

The layers are stacked in the following order, from bottom to top:
1. Camel,
2. Vanilla,
3. Vanilla,
4. Camel,
5. Vanilla,
6. Vanilla,
7. Camel,
8. Ecru
Using textile glue, glue the top of the 1st camel layer, and place the vanilla layer on top of it, making sure to position the 2 layers perfectly on top of each other, lining up the edges well.
Repeat this operation, layer after layer, for the 8 layers of the cake, finishing up with the ecru layer, with its embroidered motifs visible on top.

Cookies

🕐 30 minutes

 p. 13

Dimensions
Approximate
diameter: 1¾in
(4.5cm)

Materials
› One 2.25mm crochet hook
› DMC Happy Cotton (¾oz–47yd [20g–43m]), shade 776,
camel, ¹/₁₀oz (5g); shade 777, brown, or 754, cherry, 2¼yd (2m)

1st PART

In brown or cherry. Crochet in the round, in closed rnds.

Rnd 1: 6 sc in a magic circle; 1 sl st in the 1st st of the rnd to close it (6 st).

Rnd 2: Ch 2; 3 dc in each one of the 6 st of rnd 1; change color to camel while making the last dc; 1 sl st in the 1st dc to close (18 st).

Rnd 3: Ch 1; (1 inc, 2 sc) x 6; 1 sl st to close (24 st).

Rnd 4: (Skip 1 st, 6 dc in the next st, skip 1 st, 1 sl st in the next st) x 6, the last sl st is done in the 1st st of rnd 3 (42 st).

Mark the last dc of rnd 4. Cut the yarn to a length of 4in (10cm). Stop all the yarns on the back side.

With the camel yarn, make surface sl st all around rnd 2 (that is, around the brown or red part). To do that, insert the crochet hook in the 1st dc of rnd 2 and pull a camel yarn through this st. The crochet hook with the camel loop must be on the right side of the piece, and the starting and working yarns on the back side. Next, insert the crochet hook in the following dc and make 1 sl st on the surface. Continuing to insert the crochet hook in the dc of rnd 2, make 16 more sl st. Cut the yarn to a length of 4in (10cm) and stop it invisibly: using a needle, pull the yarn under the 2 loops of the 1st sl st, then insert the needle back where it came out, that is, in the center of the last sl st. Tie the yarns in a knot on the back side and cut them off.

2nd PART

In camel. Crochet in the round, in closed rnds.

Rnd 1: 6 sc in a magic circle; 1 sl st in the 1st st of the rnd to close it (6 st).

Rnd 2: Ch 1; 6 inc; 1 sl st to close (12 st).

Rnd 3: Ch 1; (1 sc, 1 inc) x 6; 1 sl st to close (18 st).

Rnd 4: Ch 1; (1 inc, 2 sc) x 6; 1 sl st to close (24 st).

Rnd 5: (Skip 1 st, 6 dc in the next st, skip 1 st, 1 sl st in the next st) x 6, the last sl st is made in the 1st st of rnd 4 (42 st).

Mark the 1st dc of rnd 5. Cut the yarn to a length of 20in (50cm).

ASSEMBLY

Place the 2 parts back to back, and sew them together using the yarn kept at the end of the 2nd part. Insert the needle under the 2 loops of the st marked on the 2nd part, from the right side to the back side, and under the 2 loops of the st marked on the 1st part, from the back side toward the front.

Then insert the needle under the 2 loops of the next st on the 1st part (this is the next to last dc of rnd 4), from the right side to the back side, and under the 2 loops of the next st on the 2nd part (this is the 2nd dc of rnd 5), from the back side to the front.

Continue like that all around the cookie, inserting the needle each time in the 6 dc that form the rounded parts.

Make sure not to pull the sewing st too tight to avoid deforming the edges of the cookie.

To finish, pull the yarn between the two thicknesses by going back and forth on the inside, and cut the yarn off flush with the surface.

Elephant Ear Cookies

⏱ 1 hour 15 minutes

 p. 14

Dimensions
Approximate sizes:
2⅓in x 1¾in
(6cm x 4.5cm)

Preliminary information
To avoid making the starting ch tighter than the following rows, all you need to do is use a bigger crochet hook. Personally, I crochet the ch of the starting ch with a 2.5mm crochet hook and the rest of the design with a 2.25mm crochet hook. If you don't have a crochet hook of that size, just crochet the ch rather loosely.

Materials
› One 2.25 mm crochet hook and one 2.5mm crochet hook (optional)
› DMC Happy Cotton (¾oz–47yd [20g–43m]), shade 776, camel, ¼oz (7g); shade 770, lemonade yellow, 2¾yd (2.5m)

In camel. Crochet in rows.
Row 1: Ch 56, keeping 24in (60cm) of starting yarn; 55 sc starting in the 2nd st away from the crochet hook; mark the lower loop of the ch closest to the starting slip knot; turn the work (55 st).
Row 2: Ch 1; 55 sc; turn (55 st).
Row 3: Ch 1; 55 sc; change color to yellow, while making the last sc, keeping a length of 4in (10cm) of starting yarn; turn (55 st).
Cut the camel yarn to a length of 4in (10cm).
In lemonade yellow.
Row 4: Ch 1; 55 sc; change color to camel while doing the last sc, keeping 4in (10cm) of starting yarn; turn (55 st).
Cut the lemonade yellow yarn to a length of 4in (10cm).
In camel.
Row 5: Ch 1; 55 sc; turn (55 st).
Row 6: Ch 1, 55 sc; mark the 1st sc of the row (55 st).
Cut the yarn to a length of 24in (60cm). Bring the four 4in (10cm) lengths of yarn to the inside by passing them under a few st invisibly, then cut them off flush with the surface.
Now sew the piece obtained to form a long tube. The outside face of the tube is the one that was facing you when you crocheted row 6.
Using a needle and the starting yarn, sew edge to edge from the bottom to the top of the piece, that is, sew the lower loops of the starting ch to the 2 loops of row 6. Insert the needle into the st marked at the bottom of the piece, then under the 2 loops of the st marked at the top (that is, the 1st st of row 6). Make a similar sewing st in the following 54 st, stuffing very lightly as you go along. The stuffing must allow the tube to remain rounded, but must be sufficiently light so that you can bend it into the desired shape.
It is not necessary to close the ends of the tube, because the folding will keep the stuffing from coming out.
Now fold the tube into the shape shown in the diagram. The yellow band must be on the front side of the palm tree, clearly visible and centered. First roll the 1st half and hold it in place with a pin. Do the same with the 2nd half and bring the 2 halves to the center of the palm tree.
Adjust the folding as much as necessary so that the palm tree is quite symmetrical. Hold the fold with several pins.
Using a needle that is long enough and the yarn kept at the end, make several sewing st traversing the entire piece in different directions. Remove the pins and test the solidity of the sewing. If necessary, make several more st at the points where the structure is least stable. When you are satisfied with the result, pull the yarn to the inside and cut it off flush with the surface.

Pancakes

Dimensions
Approximate
diameter: 3½in (9cm)

Preliminary information
The instructions are given for one pancake. To make them as delicious
as you would like, crochet the toppings of your choice by following the
instructions given in the *Toppings* chapter, pp. 59–63. You can crochet
the toppings separately to make a kit to assemble, or keep a length of
yarn at the end of each topping to sew it onto the pancake.

Materials
› One 2.25mm crochet hook
› DMC Happy Cotton (¾oz–47yd [20g–43 m]), shade 776, camel, ³/₅oz (16g); shade 770, lemonade
yellow, ¹/₁₀oz (3g)

1st PART
In camel. Crochet in a spiral.
Rnd 1: 7 sc in a magic circle; keep 4in (10cm) of
starting yarn (7 st).
Rnd 2: 7 inc (14 st).
Rnd 3: (1 inc, 1 sc) x 7 (21 st).
Rnd 4: (1 sc, 1 inc, 1 sc) x 7 (28 st).
Rnd 5: (1 inc, 3 sc) x 7 (35 st).
Rnd 6: (2 sc, 1 inc, 2 sc) x 7 (42 st).
Rnd 7: (1 inc, 5 sc) x 7 (49 st).
Rnd 8: (3 sc, 1 inc, 3 sc) x 7 (56 st).
Rnd 9: (1 inc, 7 sc) x 7 (63 st).
Rnd 10: (4 sc, 1 inc, 4 sc) x 7 (70 st).
Rnd 11: (1 inc, 9 sc) x 7 (77 st).
In lemonade yellow. Cut the camel yarn to a length
of 2in (5cm).
Rnd 12: (5 sc, 1 inc, 5 sc) x 7 (84 st).
Rnd 13: (1 sl st; do not crochet the other st of the
rnd (84 st).
Cut the lemonade yellow yarn to a length of 4in
(10cm) and stop it invisibly. Tie the camel and
lemonade yellow yarns together and cut them off.

2nd PART
Rnds 1 to 13: Repeat the instructions for rnds 1 to
13 of the 1st part.
Cut the yarn to a length of 28in (70cm) and
stop it invisibly. Keep the yarn to sew the 2 parts
together. Tie the yarns together at the color
change and cut them off.

ASSEMBLY
Place the two parts back to back. Using a needle
and the yarn saved at the end of the 2nd part, sew
the two thicknesses together: insert the needle in
the back loop of 1 st of the 1st part, from the back
to the front side, then in the back loop of a st of
the 2nd part, from the back to the front.
After sewing half the perimeter of the pancake,
slide a thin layer of stuffing inside. The idea is
to reproduce the "raised" side of the pancakes
without giving them too much thickness. To keep
the pancakes from losing their shape when played
with by children, tie together the 4in (10cm) of
yarn kept at the start of each part.
Continue sewing, adding a bit of stuffing as you go
along. Stop and cut the yarn off.

Rainbow Layer Cake

 3 hours 45 minutes

 p. 16

Dimensions
Approximate sizes:
3⅛in x 1¾in
(8cm x 4.5cm)

Preliminary information
The instructions and the material necessary are given for one slice, made by stacking 11 layers of cake of different colors, and 2 layers of icing. To make the entire cake, make 6 slices in all.

In the instructions for this design, "1 dec" is always made in hdc.

Technical reminder: When we crochet in half-double rows, we start by making ch 2, then we make the 1st hdc in the 2nd st of the row. The ch 2 are in fact substitute st that replace the 1st hdc. For example, in row 2, we have 17 hdc, but we count 18 st in all on the row, since the ch 2 replaces 1 hdc.

Materials
› One 2.25mm crochet hook
› DMC Happy Cotton (¾oz–47yd [20g–43m]), shade 761, ecru, 1⅛oz (33g); shade 756 violet, ⅕oz (4g); shade 786, cyan blue, ⅕oz (4g); shade 779, apple green, ⅕oz (4g); shade 788, lemon yellow, ⅕oz (4g); shade 792, orange, ⅕oz (4g); shade 799, bubblegum pink, ⅕oz (4g)
› Textile glue or hot glue

CAKE LAYER x 11

Crochet in rows. This piece is to be made 5 times in ecru, and once each in each one of the other 6 colors.

Row 1: Ch 20, keeping 4in (10cm) of starting yarn; 18 hdc starting in the 3rd st away from the crochet hook, turn the work (19 st).

Row 2: Ch 2, 17 hdc, turn (18 st).

Row 3: Ch 2, 7 hdc, 1 dec, 7 hdc, turn (16 st).

To make the dec in hdc as invisible as possible for this project, I suggest doing them like this: yarn over; insert the crochet hook under the 2 loops of the 1st st; yarn over a 2nd time; bring back the yarn through the st; insert the crochet hook under the 2 loops of the next st; yarn over a 3rd time; bring the yarn back through the st. You now have 4 loops on the crochet hook. Yarn over one more time and bring the yarn back through the 4 loops.

Row 4: Ch 1, 14 hdc, turn (15 st).

Row 5: Ch 2, 13 hdc, turn (14 st).

Row 6: Ch 2, 7 hdc, 1 dec, 3 hdc, turn (12 st).

Row 7: Ch 2, 10 hdc, turn (11 st).

Row 8: Ch 2, 2 hdc, 1 dec, 5 hdc, turn (9 st).

Row 9: Ch 2, 7 hdc, turn (8 st).

Row 10: Ch 2, 2 hdc, 1 dec, 2 hdc, turn (6 st).

Row 11: Ch 2, 4 hdc, turn (5 st).

Row 12: Ch 2, 1 dec, 1 hdc, turn (3 st).

Row 13: Ch 1, skip 1 st, 1 sc in the next st (1 st).

Make ch 1 to stop the piece, and cut the yarn to a length of 4in (10cm). Pull the starting yarns and the ending yarns to the inside by passing them under several st invisibly, then cut them off flush with the surface.

LOWER LAYER OF ICING

In ecru. Crochet in rows.

Row 1: Ch 21, keeping 4in (10cm) of starting yarn; 19 hdc starting in the 3rd st away from the crochet hook, turn the work (20 st).

Rows 2 to 6: Ch 2, 19 hdc, turn (20 st).

The last st of these rows is done by inserting the crochet hook in the upper st of the substitution ch that replaces the 1st hdc.

Row 7: Ch 2, 18 hdc, turn (19 st).
Row 8: Ch 2, 17 hdc, turn (18 st).
Row 9: Ch 2, 7 hdc, 1 dec, 7 hdc, turn (16 st).
Row 10: Ch 2, 14 hdc, turn (15 st).
Row 11: Ch 2, 13 hdc, turn (14 st).
Row 12: Ch 2, 7 hdc, 1 dec, 3 hdc, turn (12 st).
Row 13: Ch 2, 10 hdc, turn (11 st).
Row 14: Ch 2, 2 hdc, 1 dec, 5 hdc, turn (9 st).
Row 15: Ch 2, 7 hdc, turn (8 st).
Row 16: Ch 2, 2 hdc, 1 dec, 2 hdc, turn (6 st).
Row 17: Ch 2, 4 hdc, turn (5 st).
Row 18: Ch 2, 1 dec, 1 hdc, turn (3 st).
Row 19: Ch 1, skip 1 st, 1 sc in the next st (1 st).
Make ch 1 to stop the piece, and cut the yarn to a length of 4in (10cm). Pull the starting yarns and the ending yarns to the inside by passing them under several st invisibly, then cut them off flush with the surface.

UPPER LAYER OF ICING

In ecru. Crochet in rows.
Row 1: Ch 21, keeping 4in (10cm) of starting yarn; 19 hdc starting in the 3rd st from the crochet hook, turn the work (20 st).
Rows 2 to 7: Ch 2, 19 hdc, turn (20 st).
Row 8: Ch 2, 18 hdc, turn (19 st).
Row 9: Ch 2, 17 hdc, turn (18 st).
Row 10: Ch 2, 7 hdc, 1 dec, 7 hdc, turn (16 st).
Row 11: Ch 2, 14 hdc, turn (15 st).
Row 12: Ch 2, 13 hdc, turn (14 st).
Row 13: Ch 2, 7 hdc, 1 dec, 3 hdc, turn (12 st).
Row 14: Ch 2, 10 hdc, turn (11 st).
Row 15: Ch 2, 2 hdc, 1 dec, 5 hdc, turn (9 st).
Row 16: Ch 2, 7 hdc, turn (8 st).
Row 17: Ch 2, 2 hdc, 1 dec, 2 hdc, turn (6 st).
Row 18: Ch 2, 4 hdc, turn (5 st).
Row 19: Ch 2, 1 dec, 1 hdc, turn (3 st).
Row 20: Ch 1, skip 1 st, 1 sc in the next st (1 st).
Make ch 1 to stop the piece, and cut the yarn to a length of 4in (10cm). Pull the starting yarns and the ending yarns to the inside by passing them under several st invisibly, then cut them off flush with the surface.

WHIPPED CREAM

In ecru, crochet 1 element following the instructions given in the *Toppings* chapter, p. 62. Now sew the whipped cream on the upper layer of icing. It should be positioned straddling rows 10 to 12 of the icing, well centered in the middle of the triangle. Make a sewing st at the level of each dc of rnd 3 of the whipped cream, then tie a knot in the yarn on the back side of the layer of icing.

ASSEMBLY

The layers are stacked in the following order, from bottom to top:
1. Violet,
2. Ecru,
3. Cyan blue,
4. Ecru
5. Apple green,
6. Ecru,
7. Lemon yellow,
8. Ecru,
9. Orange,
10. Ecru,
11. Bubblegum pink,
12. Lower layer of icing,
13. Upper layer of icing.

Using textile glue, glue the top side of the violet layer and place the ecru layer on top of it, positioning the two layers perfectly so that the edges are well aligned.
Repeat this operation, layer after layer, for the 11 layers of the cake.
When the glue is completely dry, position the lower layer of icing using pins. On the upper part of the cake, the icing should be perfectly aligned with the other layers. On the exterior part of the cake, the layer of icing must perfectly cover the first 11 layers.
When everything is well positioned using pins, start by gluing the horizontal part of the icing, leaving the pins holding the vertical part in place; then glue the vertical part.

Once the glue is dry, glue the upper layer of icing in the same way.

According to the way you glue the 11 layers of cake, you may obtain a total height of the piece that is slightly different. If the layers of icing seem to be too big, it is possible to eliminate one row among rows 2 to 6 of the lower level of icing and one among rows 2 to 7 of the upper layer.

Common Elements of the Tarts

 50 minutes/25 minutes

 p. 17–21

In this chapter, we have two possibilities for crocheting the tarts:
Crochet the different elements and sew them together to obtain a finished object: in this case, you must crochet the specific custard for **tarts to be sewn**, and follow the appropriate instructions.
Crochet the various elements without sewing them, so that children can play with assembling the various ingredients into tarts of their choice: in this case, you must crochet the custard for **tarts to be assembled**, and follow the appropriate instructions.

Approximate times
50 minutes for the tart crust and
25 minutes for the custard

Dimensions
Approximate diameter: 3⅛in (8cm)

Preliminary information
To make the tart crust, we use sts that are a little more technical: the relief st on the front or back, and the crab st. For more instructions for the relief st, see the *Techniques* chapter, p. 26.
The crab st consists of making single crochet sts in the opposite direction from the direction you normally crochet (for right-handed crocheters, from left to right).
Start by inserting the crochet hook under 2 loops of the preceding st. Catch the working yarn at the back, by passing it under the crochet hook. Bring this yarn back through the st in which you inserted the crochet hook and bring the crochet hook above the st in which you are working, in the usual position. Make 1 yo, and pass the yarn through the 2 loops on the crochet hook. Repeat these steps to form new st.

Materials
› One 2.25mm crochet hook
› DMC Happy Cotton (¾oz–47yd [20g–43m]), **Tart crust:** shade 776, camel, ½oz (14g);
Custard: See the instructions for each tart for the shade of yarn, ⅓oz (8g)

TART CRUST

In camel. Crochet in the round, in closed rnds.
Rnd 1: 7 sc in a magic circle; 1 sl st in the 1st st of the rnd to close it (7 st).
Rnd 2: Ch 1; 7 inc; 1 sl st to close (14 st).
Rnd 3: Ch 1; (1 sc, 1 inc) x 7; 1 sl st to close (21 st).
Rnd 4: Ch 1; (1 sc, 1 inc, 1 sc) x 7; 1 sl st to close (28 st).
Rnd 5: Ch 1; (3 sc, 1 inc) x 7; 1 sl st to close (35 st).
Rnd 6: Ch 1; (2 sc, 1 inc, 2 sc) x 7; 1 sl st to close (42 st).

Rnd 7: Ch 1; (5 sc, 1 inc) x 7; 1 sl st to close (49 st).
Rnd 8: Ch 1; (3 sc, 1 inc, 3 sc) x 7; 1 sl st to close (56 st).
Rnd 9: Ch 1; (7 sc, 1 inc) x 7; 1 sc to close (64 st).
Rnd 10: Ch 1; (4 sc, 1 inc, 4 sc) x 7; 1 sl st to close (70 st).
Rnd 11: Ch 2; 70 dc relief st in back; 1 sl st in the 1st dc to close the rnd (70 st).
Contrary to what is normally done, the substitution ch at the start of this rnd are not counted as the 1st st of the rnd.

Tarts and Pies

Rnds 12 and 13: Ch 1; (1 dc relief st in front, 1 sc) x 35; 1 sl st in the 1st dc to close (70 st).
Rnd 14: Ch 1; 70 st in crab st (70 st).
For the tart to be sewn, cut the yarn to a length of 32in (80cm). Stop it invisibly and pull it through several st of the edge of the tart crust, bringing it out between rnds 9 and 10. Keep the yarn to sew the custard to the bottom of the tart.

For a tart to be assembled, cut the yarn to a length of 4in (10cm). Stop it invisibly and tie it in a discreet knot on the inside. Pull this yarn and the starting yarn under several st before cutting it off flush with the surface.

For the tart to be sewn together
Crochet in a spiral.
Rnd 1: 7 sc in a magic circle (7 st).
Rnd 2: 7 inc (14 st).
Rnd 3: (1 inc, 1 sc) x 7 (21 st).
Rnd 4: (1 sc, 1 inc, 1 sc) x 7 (28 st).
Rnd 5: (1 inc, 3 sc) x 7 (35 st).
Rnd 6: (2 sc, 1 inc, 2 sc) x 7 (42 st).
Rnd 7: (1 inc, 5 sc) x 7 (49 st).
Rnd 8: (3 sc, 1 inc, 3 sc) x 7 (56 st).
Rnd 9: (1 inc, 7 sc) x 7 (63 st).
Rnd 10: (4 sc, 1 inc, 4 sc) x 6, 4 sc, 1 inc, 3 sc, 1 sl st (70 st).
Rnd 11: 70 sl st in the back loop only (70 st).
Cut the yarn to a length of 4in (10cm). Stop it invisibly, tie it in a knot on the back side and cut.

For the tart to be assembled
Crochet in a spiral.
Rnd 1: 7 sc in a magic circle (7 st).
Rnd 2: 7 inc (14 st).
Rnd 3: (1 inc, 1 sc) x 7 (21 st).
Rnd 4: (1 sc, 1 inc, 1 sc) x 7 (28 st).
Rnd 5: (1 inc, 3 sc) x 7 (35 st).
Rnd 6: (2 sc, 1 inc, 2 sc) x 7 (42 st).
Rnd 7: (1 inc, 5 sc) x 7 (49 st).
Rnd 8: (3 sc, 1 inc, 3 sc) x 7 (56 st).

Rnd 9: (1 inc, 7 sc) x 6, 1 inc, 6 sc, 1 sl st (63 st).
Rnd 10: 63 sc in the front loop only (63 st).
Rnd 11: (10 sc, 1 inc, 10 sc) x 3 (66 st).
Rnd 12: 66 sl st in the back loop only (66 st).
Cut the yarn to a length of 4in (10cm). Stop it invisibly and tie it in a discreet knot on the outside. Pull this yarn and the starting yarn under several st before cutting them off flush with the surface.

Raspberry-Blackberry Tarts

4 hours 15 minutes / 3 hours

 p. 20

Approximate time
4 hours 15 minutes for
the tart to be sewn,
3 hours for the tart to
be assembled

Dimensions
Approximate diameter:
3⅛in (8cm)

Materials
› One 2.25mm crochet hook
› DMC Happy Cotton (¾oz–47yd [20g–43m]), shade 755, raspberry,
or 758, navy blue, ⁴/₁₀oz to ½oz (12g to 14g); shade 776, camel, ½oz
(14g); shade 764, pale pink, or 761, ecru, ½oz (8g).
› Optional: small sheet of plastic or cardboard: about 3in x 3in (7.5cm x
7.5cm). See the *Materials* chapter, p. 23, for more information.

RASPBERRIES OR BLACKBERRIES

Crochet the berries in raspberry or navy blue,
following the instructions given in the *Toppings*
chapter, p. 59.
For the tart to be sewn, you will need 14 berries,
and for the tart to be assembled, 12.

ASSEMBLY

For the tart to be sewn
Make the tart crust in camel, following the
instructions on p. 49.
Make the custard for the tart to be sewn, by
following the instructions on p. 50:
in pale pink for the raspberry tart; in ecru for the
blackberry tart.
Lightly stuff the 14 berries. To sew them more
easily to the custard, we will stitch them together
to form an exterior circle and a central square.
Thread a yarn of the same color through 4 berries,
at the level of rnd 5. Form a square by positioning
the open side of the berries facing downward. Tie
the 2 ends of the yarn together, making sure that
all the berries are stuck to each other without
being crushed. Pull each end of yarn to the inside
and cut it off flush with the surface.
Working in the same way, thread a yarn through
the remaining 10 berries to form the outside circle.
Make sure that the circle has the correct size to
surround the central square and to be sewn on to
the custard.

Position the central square around rnd 1 of the
custard, straddling rnds 2 to 5, and take a long
yarn of the same color as the berries to sew them.
Personally, I make one sewing st on each fruit, on
the inside of the square, between the st of rnds
1 and 2 of the custard; then I make 4 additional
sewing st on each fruit, on the outside of the
square. You can choose to make 1 st in each st
of each fruit, but as I see it, that is tedious and
unnecessary. Tie the starting and ending yarns
together on the back side, or continue to sew with
the same yarn.
Next, position the exterior circle around the
central square, straddling rnds 7 to 10.
Start by keeping the circle in place by making a
sewing st in each fruit, on the interior edge of the
circle. Next, make 4 sewing st on each fruit, on
the exterior edge of the circle. Stop all the sewing
yarns on the back side.
In the sheet of cardboard or plastic, cut a
circle of the same diameter as the tart crust.
Personally, I cut a circle 2⅞in (7.2cm) in
diameter, but this measurement should be
adjusted according to the yarn and crochet hook
chosen, and according to whether you crochet
more or less loosely.
Position the circle on the inside of the tart crust.
*This step is optional. If you don't add a rigid base,
make sure not to stuff the tart too much, so that the
top will remain quite flat.*

Using the yarn kept at the end of the tart crust step, sew the custard. Insert the needle under the 2 loops of the sl st of the last rnd of the custard, and in the st of rnd 10 of the tart crust, at the place where you made the relief st in back in rnd 11. After having sewn three-quarters of the tart, insert a little filling between the plastic or cardboard circle and the custard. Finish sewing, then pull the yarn to the inside by making a few st in the stuffing.

For the tart to be assembled
Make the tart crust in camel, following the instructions on p. 49.
Make the custard for the tart to be assembled, by following the instructions on p. 50:
in pale pink for the raspberry tart; in ecru for the blackberry tart.
Place the custard on the tart crust, then the 12 berries on the custard.

Blueberry Tarts

 4 hours 30 minutes / 3 hours 10 minutes

 p. 18

Approximate time
4 hours 30 minutes for the tart to be sewn, 3 hours 10 minutes for the tart to be assembled

Dimensions
Approximate diameter: 3⅛in (8cm)

Materials
› One 2.25mm crochet hook
› DMC Happy Cotton (¾oz–47 yd [20g–43m]), shade 758, navy blue, ½oz–⅔oz (16g–19g), shade 776, camel, ½oz (14g), shade 756, violet, ⅓oz (8g)
› Optional: small sheet of plastic or cardboard: about 3in x 3in (7.5cm x 7.5cm). See the *Materials* chapter, p. 23, for more information.

BLUEBERRIES

Crochet the blueberries by following the instructions given in the *Toppings* chapter, p. 59. For the tart to be sewn, you'll need to make 19 berries, and for the tart to be assembled, 16.

ASSEMBLAGE

For the tart to be sewn
Make the tart crust in camel, following the instructions on p. 49.
Make the custard for the tart to be sewn in violet, following the instructions on p. 50.
To sew the blueberries more easily to the custard, you will stitch them together to form an outside circle and a central circle.
Thread a yarn of the same color through 6 berries, at the level of rnd 3. Form a circle

by placing the 1st rnd of the blueberries toward the top. Make this circle by threading the yarn through the 1st blueberry, bringing it out again at the center of the circle, on this same blueberry. Take a 7th berry, thread the yarn through it and insert the needle in the blueberry opposite it on the circle. You will produce a circle of 6 blueberries with a 7th one in the center, all held firmly together. Stop the yarns and cut them off flush with the surface. Working in the same way, thread a yarn through the 12 remaining berries to make the outer circle. Make sure that the circle is the correct size to surround the central circle and to be sewn to the custard. Place the central round in the center of the custard and take a long length of yarn of the same color as the berries to sew them down. Personally, I make a sewing st in each berry.

Tie the starting and ending yarns in a knot on the back side, or continue to sew with the same yarn. Next, position the outer circle around this inner circle, and likewise make a sewing st in each berry. Stop all the sewing yarns on the back side.

From the piece of plastic or cardboard, cut a circle of the same diameter as the tart crust. Personally, I cut a circle 2⅞in (7.2cm) in diameter, but this measurement should be adjusted according to the yarn and crochet hook chosen, and according to whether you crochet more or less loosely.

Position the circle on the inside of the tart crust. *This step is optional. If you don't add the rigid base, make sure to not stuff the tart too much so that the bottom remains nice and flat.*

Using the yarn kept at the end of making the tart crust, sew the custard. Insert the needle under the 2 loops of the sl st of the last round of the custard and in the st of rnd 10 of the tart crust, at the place where you made the dc relief st in back of rnd 11. After having sewn three-quarters of the tart, insert a little stuffing between the plastic or cardboard circle and the custard. Finish the sewing, then make a few more st in the stuffing.

For the tart to be assembled

Make the tart crust in camel, following the instructions on p. 49.

Make the custard for the tart to be assembled in violet, following the instructions on p. 50.

Place the custard in the pie crust, then the 16 berries on the custard. You can leave the berries separate, or make an inner circle of 5 berries and an exterior circle of 11 berries, sewing the blueberries to each other, as explained for the tart to be sewn.

STRAWBERRY TART

By making a custard for the tart to be assembled in strawberry milk, and by crocheting 8 strawberries without leaves on top, you can make a strawberry tart to be assembled!

Cherry Pies

Approximate time
3 hours for the pie to be sewn, 2 hours 30 minutes for the pie to be assembled

Dimensions
Approximate diameter: 3⅛in (8cm)

Preliminary information
The filling of this pie is crocheted by alternating rnds of sc and rnds of dc and of bobble stitches (bo). To crochet a bobble stitch, make 4 tr starting in the same st and then flow them together:
- yo twice, insert the crochet hook in the st indicated;
- yo a 3rd time and pull the yarn through the st;
- yo a 4th time and pull the yarn through 2 loops;
- yo a 5th time and pull the yarn through 2 loops.
Repeat these 4 steps three more times in the same st so you have 4 tr started. Finally, yo one last time and pull the yarn through the 5 loops on the crochet hook.
Idea: By using navy blue yarn for the custard, this tart becomes an alternative to the blueberry tart!

Materials
› One 2.25mm crochet hook
› DMC Happy Cotton (¾oz–47yd [20g–43m]), shade 754, cherry, ²/₅oz (12g); shade 776, camel, ⁷/₁₀oz (20g)
› Optional: small sheet of plastic or cardboard: about 3in x 3in (7.5cm x 7.5cm). See the *Materials* chapter, p. 23, for more information.

PIE TO BE ASSEMBLED

Filling
In cherry. Crochet in closed rounds.
Contrary to the usual practice, the ch 2 at the start of rnds 2, 4, and 6 are not counted as substitution st.
Rnd 1: 7 sc in a magic circle; 1 sl st in the 1st st of the rnd to close it (7 st).
Rnd 2: Ch 2; starting in the 1st st of the preceding rnd: (1 dc and 1 bo in the same st) x 7; 1 sl st in the 1st dc of the rnd to close it (14 st).
Rnd 3: Ch 1; 14 inc; 1 sl st to close (28 st).
Rnd 4: Ch 2; starting in the 1st st of the preceding rnd: (1 dc, 1 bo) x 14; 1 sl st in the 1st dc of the rnd to close it (28 st).
Rnd 5: Ch 1; 28 inc; 1 sl st to close (56 st).
Rnd 6: Ch 2; starting in the 1st st of the preceding rnd: (1 dc, 1 bo, 1 dc) x 18, 1 dc, 1 bo; 1 sl st in the 1st dc of the rnd to close it (56 st).

Rnd 7: 55 sl st (56 st).
Cut the yarn to a length of 4in (10cm). Stop it invisibly and tie it in a discreet knot on the back side. Pull this yarn and the starting yarn under several st before cutting them off flush with the surface.

Pie crust
Make the tart crust in camel, following the instructions on p. 49.

Lattice top crust
Perimeter
In camel. Crochet in closed rnds.
Ch 63, then 1 sl st in the 1st st of the chain to form a large ring, making sure not to twist the ch.
Rnd 1: Ch 1; inserting the crochet hook in the upper loops of the ch: (4 sc, 1 inc, 4 sc) x 7; 1 sl st to close the rnd (70 st).

Mark the lower loop of the 1st st of the ch and leave this marker in place for as long as it takes to make the lattices. Also mark the lower loop of the 3rd st of the ch.

Rnd 2: (Ch 3, skip 1 st, 1 sl in the next st) x 35 (70 st).

Cut the yarn to a length of 4in (10cm). Stop it invisibly and tie a discreet knot on the back side. Pull this yarn and the starting yarn under several st before cutting them off flush with the surface.

Lattice top

The diagram below shows how to arrange and weave the various crosspieces. The perimeter is presented with the backside of the st facing the reader, and the marker placed in the lower loop of the 1st st of the ch is the point of reference for counting the st in which to insert the crochet hook on the perimeter.

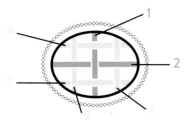

In camel. When inserting the crochet hook in the perimeter, always insert the hook from the back side toward the front side, and in the lower loops of the starting ch. As you make the various crosspieces, refer to the diagram so that you can do the weaving correctly.

1st crosspiece (shown in pink): Pull a yarn through the 3rd lower loop previously marked on the perimeter, keeping a length of 4in (10cm) of starting yarn, and make: 1 chain of ch 20, 1 sl st in the 36th st of the perimeter, 1 sl st in the 35th st, 20 sc in the upper loops of the ch that you just made, 1 sl st in the 4th st of the perimeter.
Cut the yarn to a length of 4in (10cm). Work in the starting and ending yarns after making each

crosspiece: go back and forth under a few st, invisibly, and cut off flush with the surface.

2nd central crosspiece (shown in pink): Pull a yarn through the 19th st on the perimeter and make: 1 chain of ch 20, 1 sl st in the 51st st of the perimeter, 1 sl st in the 50th st, 20 sc in the upper loops of the ch that you just made, 1 sl st in the 20th st of the perimeter.

1st lateral crosspiece (shown in green): Pull a yarn through the 30th st on the perimeter and make: 1 chain of ch 17, 1 sl st in the 9th st of the perimeter, 1 sl st in the 8th st, 17 sc in the upper loops of the ch that you just made, 1 sl st in the 31st st of the perimeter.

2nd lateral crosspiece (shown in green): Pull a yarn through the 40th st on the perimeter and make: 1 chain of ch 17, 1 sl st in the 62nd st of the perimeter, 1 sl st in the 61st st, 17 sc in the upper loops of the ch that you just made, 1 sl st in the 41st st of the perimeter.

3rd lateral crosspiece (shown in green): Pull a yarn through the 45th st of the perimeter and make: 1 chain of ch 17, 1 sl st in the 26th st of the perimeter, 1 sl st in the 25th st, 17 sc in the upper loops of the ch that you just made, 1 sl st in the 46th st of the perimeter.

4th lateral crosspiece (shown in green): Pull a yarn through the 56th st of the perimeter and make: 1 chain of ch 17, 1 sl st in the 14th st of the perimeter, 1 sl st in the 13th st, 17 sc in the upper loops of the ch that you just made, 1 sl st in the 57th st of the perimeter.

PIE TO BE SEWN

Filling

In cherry. Crochet in closed rounds.

Rnds 1 to 6: Repeat the instructions for rnds 1 to 6 of the filling for the cherry pie to be assembled, p. 54.

Rnd 7: Ch 1; (3 sc, 1 inc) x 14 (70 st).

Cut the yarn to a length of 4in (10cm). Stop it invisibly, tie it in a knot on the back side and cut it off.

Pie crust

In camel. Follow the instructions for rnds 1 to 13 of the tart crust, p. 49, without making the last sl st that closes rnd 13.

Cut the yarn to a length of 32in (80cm). Stop it invisibly and thread it under several st of the edge of the pie crust, bringing it out again between rnds 9 and 10.

In the sheet of cardboard or plastic, cut a circle of the same diameter as the pie crust. Personally, I cut a circle 2⅞in (7.2cm) in diameter, but this measurement should be adjusted according to the yarn and crochet hook chosen, and according to whether you crochet more or less loosely.

Position the circle on the inside of the pie crust. *This step is optional. If you don't add a rigid base, make sure not to stuff the pie too much, so that the bottom remains quite flat.*

Using the yarn kept at the end of the pie crust, sew the filling. Insert the needle under the 2 loops of the st of the last round of the custard and in the st of rnd 10 of the pie crust, at the place where you made the relief st in back of rnd 11. After having sewn three-quarters of the pie, insert a bit of stuffing between the plastic or cardboard circle and the filling. Finish the sewing, then bring the yarn to the inside by making a few st in the stuffing.

Lattice top crust

Follow the instructions for the perimeter and the crosspieces given for the pie to be assembled, but leaving the 2nd rnd of the perimeter waiting.

At the end of rnd 1, simply place a marker in the loop that is on the crochet hook, to secure the work, and leave the yarn waiting until you make all the crosspieces.

Then make rnd 2 of the perimeter by crocheting the perimeter together with the pie crust. For each sl st of rnd 2, insert the crochet hook under the 2 loops of the st of rnd 1 of the perimeter, then under the back loop of the st of rnd 13 of the pie crust (by inserting the crochet hook from the inside of the pie toward the outside).

Lemon Tarts

Approximate time
3 hours for the tart to be sewn, 2 hours 30 minutes for the tart to be assembled

Dimensions
Approximate diameter: 3⅛in (8cm)

Materials
› One 2.25mm crochet hook
› DMC Happy Cotton (¾ oz–47 yd [20g–43m]), shade 776, camel, ½oz (14g); shade 787, vanilla, ⅓oz (8g); shade 770, lemonade yellow, ¼oz (6g); shade 762, white, ⅓oz (9g); shade 788, lemon, ¹⁄₁₀oz (2g)
› Optional: small sheet of plastic or cardboard: about 3in x 3in (7.5cm x 7.5cm). See the *Materials* chapter, p. 23, for more information.

TOPPINGS

Crochet the toppings by following the instructions given in the *Toppings* chapter, pp. 60 and 62.
For the **tart to be sewn,** make 2 half-slices of lemon and 2 meringue peaks.
For the **tart to be assembled,** you can choose 2 half-slices of lemon and 3 meringue peaks, or 3 half-slices of lemon and 3 meringue peaks.

ASSEMBLY

For the tart to be sewn
Make the tart crust in camel, following the instructions on p. 49.
Make the custard for the tart to be sewn in vanilla, following the instructions on p. 50.
Test the positioning of the toppings by placing the custard in the tart crust without sewing it. Sew the half-slices with a few sewing st to keep them in the desired position. Sew the base of the meringue peaks at the level of the dc of rnd 3. Do not hesitate to put the custard back in the crust to see the final result.
Once all the toppings are sewn in the desired positions, tie all the sewing yarns in in knots on the back side and cut off the excess yarn.
From the piece of plastic or cardboard, cut a circle of the same diameter as the tart crust. Personally, I cut a circle 2⅞in (7.2cm) in diameter, but this measurement should be adjusted according to the

yarn and crochet hook chosen, and according to whether you crochet more or less loosely.
Position the circle on the inside of the tart crust. *This step is optional. If you don't add the rigid base, make sure not to stuff the tart too much, so that the bottom remains nice and flat.*
Using the yarn kept at the end of making the tart crust, sew the custard. Insert the needle under the 2 loops of the sl st of the last round of the custard and in the st of rnd 10 of the tart crust, at the place where you made the dc relief st in front of rnd 11. After having sewn three-quarters of the tart, insert a little stuffing between the plastic or cardboard circle and the custard. Finish the sewing, then make a few more st in the stuffing.

For the tart to be assembled
Make the tart crust in camel, following the instructions on p. 49.
Make the custard for the tart to be assembled in vanilla, following the instructions on p. 50.
Place the custard in the tart crust, then the toppings on the custard.

Fruit Tarts

Approximate time
4 hours 45 minutes
for the tart to be sewn,
3 hours 30 minutes
for the tart to be
assembled

Dimensions
Approximate
diameter: 3⅛in (8cm)

Materials
› One 2.25mm crochet hook
› DMC Happy Cotton (¾oz–47yd [20g–43m]), shade 776, camel, ½oz
(14g), lemonade yellow, ⅓oz (8g); **Raspberries:** shade 755, raspberry,
¹/₁₀oz (2g); **Blackberry + blueberry:** shade 758, navy blue, ¹/₁₀oz (2g);
Strawberries: shade 789, red, ¼oz (6g); Orange: shade 792, orange, ¹/₁₀oz
(3g); **Orange + kiwis:** shade 762, white, ¹/₁₀oz (2g); **Kiwis:** shade 779,
apple green, ³/₂₀oz (4g)
› DMC Pearl Cotton, size 5, shade white, (1.5m) (strawberries); shade
black, 39in (1m) (kiwis)
› Optional: small sheet of plastic or cardboard: about 3in x 3in (7.5cm x
7.5cm). See the *Materials* chapter, p. 23, for more information.

FRUITS

Crochet the fruits by following the instructions
given in the *Toppings* chapter, pp. 59 to 61.
To make the same tart as in the photo, make: 2
raspberries, 1 blackberry, 1 blueberry, 3 strawberries
without leaves, 1 half-slice of orange, and 2 half-slices of
kiwi. Of course, you can design your own arrangement
by mixing the fruits any way you would like!

ASSEMBLY

For the tart to be sewn
Make the tart crust in camel, following the
instructions on p. 49.
Make the custard for the tart to be sewn in lemonade
yellow, following the instructions on p. 50.
Make a trial of positioning the toppings by placing
the custard in the tart crust without sewing it.
I start by sewing the largest fruits, that is, the half-
slices of kiwi and orange. Make several sewing st on
each slice to maintain them in the desired position.
I next sew the base of the strawberries and of the
raspberry upside down, stuffing them lightly. I
finish with the blackberry and the raspberry placed
with the open side visible, and the blueberry.
At each step, do not hesitate to put the custard
back into the tart crust, to see the final result.
Once all the fruits are sewn in the desired

positions, tie knots in the sewing threads on the
back side and cut them off.
From the piece of plastic or cardboard, cut a circle
of the same diameter as the tart crust. Personally,
I cut a circle 2⅞in (7.2cm) in diameter, but this
measurement should be adjusted according to the
yarn and crochet hook chosen, and according to
whether you crochet more or less loosely.
Position the circle on the inside of the tart crust.
*This step is optional. If you don't add the rigid base,
make sure not to stuff the tart too much, so that the
bottom remains nice and flat.*
Using the yarn kept at the end of making the tart
crust, sew the custard. Insert the needle under
the 2 loops of the sl st of the last round of the
custard and in the st of rnd 10 of the tart crust, at
the place where you made the dc relief st in front
of rnd 11. After having sewn three-quarters of the
tart, insert a little stuffing between the plastic or
cardboard circle and the custard. Finish the sewing,
then make a few more st in the stuffing.

For the tart to be assembled
Make the tart crust in camel, following the
instructions on p. 49.
Make the custard for the tart to be sewn in lemonade
yellow, following the instructions on p. 50.
Place the custard in the tart crust, then the 10
fruits on the custard, as you like.

Berries

Dimensions
Approximate
height: ½in to 1½in
(1.5cm to 3.5cm)

Materials
› One 2.25mm crochet hook
› DMC Happy Cotton (¾oz–47yd [20g–43m]), **Raspberry:** shade
755, raspberry, ¹/₂₀oz (1g); **Blackberry:** shade 758, navy blue, ¹/₂₀oz (1g);
Blueberry: shade 758, navy blue, ¹/₂₀oz (1g); **Strawberry:** shade 789, red,
¹/₁₀oz (2g); shade 781, malachite green, 39in (1m)
› DMC Pearl Cotton, size 5, white, 20in (50cm) per strawberry

RASPBERRY/BLACKBERRY

In raspberry or navy blue. Crochet in a spiral.
Rnd 1: 6 sc in a magic circle (6 st).
Rnd 2: (1 sc, 1 inc BLO) x 3 (9 st).
Rnd 3: (1 sc, 1 sc BLO) x 4, 1 sc (9 st).
Rnd 4: 1 sc BLO, 1 inc, 1 sc BLO, 1 sc, 1 inc BLO, 1 sc, 1 sc BLO, 1 inc, 1 sc BLO (12 st).
Rnd 5: (1 sc, 1 sc BLO) x 6 (12 st).
Rnd 6: (1 sl st, 1 sl st BLO) x 6 (12 st).
For the charlotte russe, the raspberry and cream macaron, the raspberry éclair, and the fruit tart to be sewn, cut the yarn to a length of 10in (25cm), stop it invisibly, and keep the length for sewing.
For the other designs, cut the yarn to a length of 4in (10cm), and stop it invisibly. Tie a knot on the inside and cut it off.

BLUEBERRY

In navy blue. Crochet in a spiral.
Rnd 1: 6 sc in a magic circle (6 st).
Rnd 2: 6 inc in the back loop only (BLO) (12 st).
Rnd 3: 12 sc (12 st).
Rnd 4: 6 dec (6 st).
Stuff.
For the charlotte russe and the fruit tart to be sewn, cut the yarn to a length of 10in (25cm), close, and keep the yarn for sewing.
For the other designs, cut the yarn to a length of 6in (15cm) and close the piece. Stop the yarn by making several st and cut it off flush with the surface.

STRAWBERRY

Berry
In red. Crochet in a spiral.
Rnd 1: 6 sc in a magic circle (6 st).
Rnd 2: (1 inc, 1 sc) x 3 (9 st).
Rnd 3: 9 sc (9 st).
Rnd 4: (1 sc, 1 inc, 1 sc) x 3 (12 st).
Rnd 5: 12 sc (12 st).
Rnd 6: (1 inc, 3 sc) x 3 (15 st).
Rnd 7: 15 sc (15 st).
Rnd 8: (1 dec, 1 sc) x 5 (10 st).
Stuff.
Rnd 9: 5 dec (5 st).
Mark the front loop of the last st of rnd 9.
Cut the yarn to a length of 10in (25cm). Using a needle, close the piece, by inserting the needle only under the back loops of the st of the last rnd.
For the charlotte russe, the French strawberry cake, and the fruit tart to be sewn, bring the yarn out at the level of rnd 8 of the strawberry, and keep the length for sewing.
For the other designs, stop the yarn by making several sewing st and cut off flush with the surface. Using a fine needle and the white Pearl Cotton thread, embroider small vertical lines at random over all the surface of the strawberry.

Cap
For the strawberry tart to be assembled and the fruit tart (to be sewn or to be assembled), do not crochet the cap.

For the other designs, in malachite green, crochet the cap in the front loops of rnd 9 of the strawberry. Insert the crochet hook under the previously marked front loop, inserting it from the top toward the bottom of the strawberry. Pull a malachite green yarn through, keeping 4in (10cm) of starting yarn and make: (Ch 2, 1 sl st in the 2nd st away from the crochet hook, 1 sl st in the next red st) x 4, ch 2, 1 sl st in the 2nd st away from the crochet hook.

Cut the yarn to a length of 4in (10cm). Pull the starting and ending yarns to the inside.

Sliced Fruits

🕐 15 to 20 minutes

Dimensions
Approximate diameter: 1⅛in to 2in (3cm to 5cm)

Materials
› One 2.25mm crochet hook
› DMC Happy Cotton (¾oz–47yd [20g–43m]), **Lemon:** shade 770, lemonade yellow, ¹⁄₁₀oz (2g); shade 762, white, 2¼yd (2m); **Orange:** shade 792, orange, ¹⁄₁₀oz (2g); shade 762, white, 2¼yd (2m); **Kiwi:** shade 779, apple green, ¹⁄₁₀oz (2g); shade 762, white, 60in (1.5m); **Banana:** shade 770, lemonade yellow, ¹⁄₁₀oz (2g)
› DMC Pearl Cotton, size 5, **Banana:** shade 3045, camel (or any other shade in the brown/beige range), 12in (30cm); **Kiwi:** shade black, 20in (50cm)
› Optional: textile glue or hot glue

HALF-SLICE OF LEMON OR ORANGE

Crochet in the round, in closed rounds. The sl st that closes each rnd and the ch that starts each rnd are not indicated in the instructions, for easier readability, **but you must make them for every rnd.** For more instructions, see the *Techniques* chapter, p. 24.

To make a clean color change between 2 rnds, change color while making the last sc of the rnd. The sl st that closes the rnd and the ch that start the following rnd are thus made in the new color.

In lemonade yellow/orange.

Rnd 1: 7 sc in a magic circle (7 st).
Rnd 2: 7 inc (14 st).
Rnd 3: (1 sc, 1 inc) x 7 (21 st).
Rnd 4: (1 sc, 1 inc, 1 sc) x 7 (28 st).

In white. Stop the lemonade yellow yarn. Keep the orange yarn for later use.

Rnd 5: (3 sc, 1 inc) x 7 (35 st).

In lemonade yellow/orange. Cut the white yarn to a length of 12in (30cm).

Rnd 6: (2 sc, 1 inc, 2 sc) x 7 (42 st).

Cut the lemonade yellow/orange yarn to a length of 16in (40cm).

Using the white yarn, embroider 6 lines in a star, starting from the starting magic circle, straddling rnds 1 to 4. Start by inserting the needle in the 2nd or 3rd st of rnd 4, so as to have 3 white lines clearly visible on each half of the slice.

Stop the white yarn.

Fold the slice in two, so that the lemonade yellow/orange yarn you previously set aside is now at one end. *Note: if you want the half-slice to remain very flat and not lose its shape, glue the 2 halves together with the fabric glue or the hot glue before doing the sewing.*

Using lemonade yellow/orange yarn, sew the two thicknesses edge to edge: insert the needle in the back loop of the 1st st at one of the ends, from the outside to the inside, and then the back loop of the 1st st that faces it, from the inside to the outside. Sew all the st like that, two by two.

For the lemon tart to be sewn and the fruit tart to be sewn, keep the length of yarn remaining to sew the half-slice.

For the other designs, stop the yarn by making several st and cutting it off flush with the surface.

Crochet in the round around a starting chain, in closed rnds. The sl st that closes each rnd and the ch that starts each rnd are not indicated in the instructions, to make them more readable, **but you must make them for each rnd.** For more instructions, see the *Techniques* chapter, p. 24. In order to make a crisp color change between 2 rnds, change the color while making the last sc of the rnd. The sl st that closes the rnd and the ch that start the next rnd are thus made in the new color. In white.

Rnd 1: Ch 6; 4 sc starting in the 2nd st away from the crochet hook; in the last st of the chain: 3 sc; working back up the other side of the chain: 3 sc, 1 inc (12 st).

Rnd 2: 1 inc, 3 sc, 3 inc, 3 sc, 2 inc (18 st).
In apple green. Stop the white yarn.

Rnd 3: 1 sc, 1 inc, 3 sc, (1 sc, 1 inc) x 3, 3 sc, (1 sc, 1 inc) x 2 (24 st).

Rnd 4: 1 inc, 5 sc, (1 inc, 2 sc) x 3, 3 sc, (1 inc, 2 sc) x 2 (30 st).

Rnd 5: 2 sc, 1 inc, 4 sc, (2 sc, 1 inc, 1 sc) x 3, 3 sc, (2 sc, 1 inc, 1 sc) x 2 (36 st).

Rnd 6: 1 sc, 1 inc, 6 sc, (1 sc, 1 inc, 3 sc) x 3, 3 sc, (1 sc, 1 inc, 3 sc) x 2 (42 st).

Cut the yarn to a length of 4in (10cm). Stop it invisibly, tie it in a knot on the back side and cut it off. With the black Pearl Cotton, embroider small, irregular lines straddling rnds 3 and 4, going from the center toward the exterior of the oval. Tie the starting and ending yarns together on the back side and cut them off.

Fold the slice in half such that the fold crosses the middle of the starting chain.

Note: if you want the half slice to remain flat and not lose its shape, glue the 2 halves together with fabric glue or hot glue before doing the sewing.

Using a 20in (50cm) length of apple green yarn, sew the two thicknesses edge to edge, keeping 4in (10cm) of starting yarn: insert the needle in the back loop of the 1st st at one of the ends, from the outside to the inside, then in the back loop of the 1st facing st, from the inside to the outside. Continue sewing all the st the same way, two by two. Bring the starting yarn of the sewing to the inside and cut it off flush with the surface.

For the fruit tart to be sewn, keep 12in (30cm) of yarn to sew the half-slice.

For the other designs, stop the yarn by making a few st and cutting it off flush with the surface.

1st part
In lemonade yellow. Crochet in a spiral.
Rnd 1: 6 sc in a magic circle (6 st).
Rnd 2: 6 inc (12 st).
Rnd 3: (1 sc, 1 inc) x 6 (18 st).
Rnd 4: (1 inc, 2 sc) x 6 (24 st).
Rnd 5: 1 sc, 1 sl st, do not crochet the other st of the rnd (24 st).

Cut the yarn to a length of 4in (10cm) and stop it invisibly. Tie it in a knot on the back side and cut it off.

With the camel Pearl Cotton, embroider 6 small lines straddling rnd 2, going from the center toward the outside of the circle. Tie the starting and ending yarn together on the back side and cut it off.

2nd part
In lemonade yellow. Crochet in a spiral.
Rnds 1 to 5: Repeat the instructions of the 1st part.
Cut the yarn to a length of 12in (30cm) and stop it invisibly. Keep the length for sewing the 2 parts together.
Embroider 6 lines in camel Pearl Cotton on this part, as you did on the 1st part.

Assembly
Place the 2 parts back to back. Using a needle and the yarn saved at the end of the 2nd part, sew the two thicknesses together: insert the needle in the back loop of one st of the 1st part, from the right side to the back side, then in the back loop of a st of the 2nd part, from the back side toward the front side.
Sew like this all around, then pull the yarn between the two thicknesses, go back and forth, and cut the yarn off flush with the surface.

Toppings

Delicacies

 15 to 30 minutes

Dimensions
Approximate
diameter: 1in to 2¾in
(2.5cm to 7cm)

Materials
› One 2.25mm crochet hook
› DMC Happy Cotton (¾oz–47 yd [20g–43m]), **Whipped cream/ Meringue:** shade 761, ecru, ¹/₁₀oz (3g); **Chantilly (sweetened whipped cream):** shade 762, white, ¼oz (7g); **Coulis:** shade of your choice, ¹/₅oz (5g); **Scoop of ice cream:** shade of your choice, ³/₂₀oz (4g)

WHIPPED CREAM/MERINGUE

For more instructions regarding the relief st, see the *Techniques* chapter, p. 26.
In ecru for the rainbow layer cake and in white for the lemon tart. Crochet in a spiral.
Rnd 1: 6 sc in a magic circle (6 st).
Rnd 2: 6 inc (12 st).
Rnd 3: (1 dc and 1 sc in the same st, 1 dc, 1 sc and 1 dc in the same st, 1 sc) x 3 (18 st).
Rnds 4 and 5: (1 dc relief st in front, 1 sc) x 9 (18 st).
Rnd 6: (1 dc relief st in front, skip 1 st) x 9 (9 st).
Rnd 7: 9 dc relief st in front (9 st).
Stuff lightly.
Rnd 8: 1 dc relief st in front, (skip 1 dc, 1 dc relief st in front) x 4 (5 st).
To close the piece, skip 1 dc and make 1 sl st relief st in front in the following st.
For the rainbow layer cake and the lemon tart to be sewn, cut the yarn to a length of 12in (30cm). Using a needle, bring the yarn out at the base of the piece, at the level of one of the dc of rnd 3.
For the other designs, cut the yarn to a length of 6in (15cm), stop it by making a few more st, then cut it off flush with the surface.

CHANTILLY (SWEETENED WHIPPED CREAM)

In white. Crochet in the round, in closed rounds.
Rnd 1: 7 sc in a magic circle; 1 sl st in the 1st st of the rnd to close it (7 st).
Rnd 2: Ch 1, 7 inc; 1 sl st to close (14 st).

Rnd 3: Ch 1; (1 sc, 1 inc) x 7; 1 sl st to close (21 st).
Rnd 4: Ch 1; (1 sc, 1 inc, 1 sc) x 7; 1 sl st to close (28 st).
Rnd 5: Ch 1; (3 sc, 1 inc) x 7; 1 sl st to close (35 st).
Rnd 6: Ch 1; (2 sc, 1 inc, 2 sc) x 7; 1 sl st to close (42 st).
Rnd 7: Ch 4; in the front loop only:
(1 bo, 1 hdc, 1 ch) x 21 (63 st).
To crochet a bo, make 5 tr starting in the same st and then flow them together:
- yo twice, insert the crochet hook in the st indicated;
- yo a 3rd time and pull the yarn through the st;
- yo a 4th time and pull the yarn through 2 loops;
- yo a 5th time and pull the yarn through 2 loops.
Repeat these 4 steps 4 more times in the same st so as to have 5 tr started. Finally, yo one last time and pull the yarn through the 6 loops on the crochet hook.
Cut the yarn to a length of 4in (10cm), stop it invisibly, and tie it in a knot on the back side. Pull the starting and ending yarns under a few st before cutting them off flush with the surface.

COULIS

In the color chosen. Crochet in a spiral.
Rnd 1: 7 sc in a magic circle (7 st).
Rnd 2: 7 inc (14 st).
Rnd 3: (1 sc, 1 inc) x 7 (21 st).
Rnd 4: (1 sc, 1 inc, 1 sc) x 7 (28 st).
Rnd 5: (3 sc, 1 inc) x 7 (35 st).

Rnd 6: (2 sc, 1 inc, 2 sc) x 7 (42 st).
Rnd 7: 1 sc, 1 hdc, 3 dc, 2 hdc in 1 st, 1 sc, 3 sl st, 1 hdc, 2 hdc in 1 st, 1 hdc, 1 sl st, 2 sc, 1 sl st; ch 5, starting in the 2nd st away from the crochet hook: 1 sl st, 2 sc, 1 hdc, skip 1 st on rnd 6, 1 sl st in the next st; 1 sl st, 2 sc, 1 hdc, 2 hdc in 1 st, 1 sc, 1 sl st; ch 7, starting in the 3rd st away from the crochet hook: 5 hdc, skip 2 st on rnd 6, 1 sl st in the following st; ch 11, starting in the 3rd st away from the crochet hook: 9 hdc, skip 2 st on rnd 6, 1 sl st in the next st; 2 sc; ch 6, starting in the 3rd st away from the crochet hook: 4 sc, 1 sc in the next st on rnd 6; 1 sc, ch 4; starting in the 3rd st away from the crochet hook: 2 sc, 1 sc in the next st on rnd 6; 3 sc, 3 sl st (64 st).
Cut the yarn to a length of 4in (10cm) and stop it invisibly. Tie it in a discreet knot on the back side, and pull the starting and ending yarns under a few st before cutting them off flush with the surface. If you want to sew the coulis, keep a 24in (60cm) length of yarn.
Note: So that the flows remain quite flat and do not curl up, block the work. To do that, pin the piece and the flows on a flat surface. Place them in the desired position and pin them with rustproof pins.
Then use an iron and steam them for 1 to 2 minutes, holding the iron at 2in (5cm) above the coulis, using the steam setting (if you don't have an iron, spray the piece with water). Let it dry completely before removing the pins.

SCOOP OF ICE CREAM

In the color chosen. Crochet in a spiral.
Rnd 1: 6 sc in a magic circle (6 st).
Rnd 2: 6 inc (12 st).
Rnd 3: (1 sc, 1 inc) x 6 (18 st).
Rnd 4: (1 sc, 1 inc, 1 sc) x 6 (24 st).
Rnd 5: (3 sc, 1 inc, 4 sc) x 3 (27 st).
Rnd 6: (8 sc, 1 inc) x 3 (30 st).
Rnds 7 to 10: 30 sc (30 st).
Rnd 11: (3 sc, 1 dec) x 6 (24 st).
Rnd 12: In the back loop only: (1 sc, 1 dec) x 8 (16 st).
Start to stuff.
Rnd 13: 8 dec (8 st).

Finish stuffing, keeping the bottom quite flat. Cut the yarn to a length of 12in (30cm) and close. Keep the length if you wish to sew the scoop of ice cream. Otherwise, pull the yarn to the inside and cut it off flush with the surface.